The Future of Light

GW00692120

The Future of Light

Hardwin Tibbs

Watkins
London & Dulverton

© 1981 B C H Tibbs

First edition 1981

British Library CIP Data
Tibbs, B.C. Hardwin
   The future of light.
   1. Light — Physiological effects.
   I. Title
   613'.19   QH545/

ISBN 0 7224 0196 5

Watkins Publishing
Bridge Street, Dulverton
Somerset TA22 9HJ

Watkins Bookshop
21 Cecil Court, Charing Cross Road
London WC2N 4HB

Printed in Great Britain by
A Wheaton & Co Ltd, Exeter
Cover and diagrams by B C H Tibbs

Contents

Preface

Many of the findings reported in this book are still controversial. They have been carefully set in a wider perspective to permit them a fair hearing for the first time.

The book is intended to be scientifically and technically authoritative, but it is written as far as possible to be understood by the general reader: all the principal scientific terms are defined where they first appear. I hope it will be read not only by all those who have an interest in the factors that influence our health, but also by those working in the lighting industry and in photobiology, for whom it poses some problematical but challenging questions.

International recognition of the issue encapsulated in this book is slowly coming. The Commission Internationale de l'Eclairage (CIE) now has a special committee reviewing the photobiological effects of lighting, and in West Germany a national standard, DIN 5031, November 1979, describing the spectral distribution requirements for 'photobiologically effective' lighting has been drawn up by the Deutsches Institut für Normung.

Between the time this is written and the end of the century, the ideas presented here will be thoroughly researched, discussed and perhaps implemented on a worldwide scale if we want our surroundings truly to ensure our good health. My hope is that this book will act as a catalyst in that process.

Acknowledgements

My interest in the subject of this book began with a lecture given by David Garlovsky in London in 1977, and was confirmed by a visit to Dr John Ott in Florida in 1978. I thank especially Michael Frye, Chairman of Concord Rotaflex in London, for his enthusiasm and support during the research I subsequently undertook, which was partly sponsored by The Light and Health Research Council. I also thank Professor I.A. Magnus at the Institute of Dermatology in London for his valuable criticism of an early draft of this book.

Spectral data for the fluorescent lamp curves in Figure 6 were prepared at Trinity and All Saints' Colleges, Leeds, by Dr Michael Potter and David Simpson. I thank David Simpson for devising and implementing the data-processing which was required. The lamps measured were a Thorn 'White' and a Duro-Test 'True-Lite' (the 'True-Lite' is marketed as 'Vita-Lite' in the United States).

The transmission curve for float glass shown in Figure 5 was supplied by Pilkington Brothers, Lancashire. The curve for ultraviolet-transmitting 'Plexiglas' acrylic-sheet was supplied by Rohm and Haas, Pennsylvania. Figure 3 is based on two similar diagrams in Haber and Hershenson (1973). The rod and cone detail in Figure 2 in fact shows these cells as found in the retina of the Salamander *Necturus* (after Brown P.K. et al (1963) J. Cell. Biol. 19, p79).

Introduction

Not all our seeing is for sight.

The light which enters our eyes and allows us to see also triggers changes deep in our nervous system, altering the pattern of our hormone production and the process of our internal biochemistry, affecting as a result not only our mood but even our health.

As the scientific evidence gradually accumulates there is a growing suspicion that much contemporary artificial lighting is actually having a detrimental effect on the biochemical poise of our bodies and may even be contributing to the ill-health of modern society as much as cigarette smoking or diets high in animal fats are believed to be doing. Indeed, it may be that 'mal-illumination', as this condition has been called, is actually exacerbating some of the cancer and heart disease which has previously been attributed to these other two causes. Moreover, while we have some measure of choice as to whether we smoke or not and about what we eat, the artificial lighting we are exposed to is very often not a matter for individual choice.

The evidence behind these remarkable assertions about the biological role of light has come from America, but it is finding support from scientific work in Europe and Russia. Although it has been a matter of controversy for many years, it is now clear that by means of channels reaching from the eye to the involuntary part of the nervous system, light does affect the secretion of hormones by the principal endocrine glands, which in turn affect chemical activity throughout the body. It is also becoming increasingly apparent that the colour of the light, or mixture of colours in the light, is crucial in determining whether this influence is beneficial or harmful to our health.

As so often before, we find that the ingredients of our natural environment cannot be substituted haphazardly. In this case, it seems that natural sunlight provides precisely what is needed to ensure the optimum biochemical balance in our bodies. Perhaps this is not surprising since we evolved over millions of years under natural sunlight, so that those parts of our biology which are sensitive to light are now uniquely adapted to the characteristic mixture of wavelengths in daylight.

The idea that sunlight is important, or even essential for life is not really new: the opening verses of the Bible make it clear that light featured very early in the scheme of creation it describes. What is ironic is that it is only the invention and deployment of electric artificial lighting in the last hundred years which has enabled us to appreciate fully the extent of our dependence on daylight, and the risks we run if we cut ourselves off from it. We use artificial lighting on a vast scale, many of us spending most of our waking hours under such lighting, so it is now imperative that we thoroughly explore and understand our biological responses to electric light and daylight, and even to daylight seen through glass.

The lighting industry has already developed light sources

which approach natural daylight in their colour output:
now we need to develop an awareness of their importance.
This book presents the arguments that confront us and challenge us to devise strategies for artificial lighting that will
meet the needs of our bodies, not just our eyes.

The Nature of Light

The picture most of us have of light is that it is something entirely external to us: a form of energy bouncing about in the outside world to which we respond with two camera-like organs in our heads that let us find our way around.

As far as it goes, this picture is accurate. Light is a form of 'electromagnetic' energy, just as radio waves are. This is radiation with both an electrical and a magnetic component, which travels through empty space at literally 'the speed of light', a speed so high, 186,000 miles a *second*, that it is hard to grasp mentally. The sun is 93 million miles away, but its light takes only 8½ minutes to reach us.

All the useful light in our natural environment comes from the sun (including moonlight, since the moon has no light of its own and simply reflects part of the sunlight that falls on it). Apart from this, the only other natural sources of light, such as lightning strikes, fire, or the aurora borealis are too dim, brief or infrequent to be of much general importance. Our sun is the nearest star, and its chief function from our point of view is to radiate a vast amount of electromagnetic energy which happens to be most intense at just those wavelengths we see as light.

The concept of wavelength is important and we return to it frequently in this book. Light can be imagined as spreading out from its source like the ripples on a pond when a stone is thrown in. This is at best a mental sketch, since the light waves can spread out in three dimensions and the question of what it is that waves or vibrates goes well beyond the scope of this book. Furthermore, only one size of wave is produced in the pond, whereas electromagnetic waves can be transmitted in a vast range of sizes simultaneously. What we see as light is a single octave of electromagnetic waves with a peak-to-peak wave size or wavelength in the order of a few ten-thousandths of a millimetre. If this range of wavelengths is spread out or arranged in order of increasing wave size, as by passing sunlight through a prism, a spectrum of colours is produced and the colours are those of the rainbow. If this sequence of wavelengths could be extended to include the whole gamut of electromagnetic radiation it would result in a much larger spectrum extending invisibly on either side of the part we see as light.

'Below' visible light at longer wavelengths there would be first the invisible infrared radiation which we feel as heat ('infra' is the Latin for 'below'). The infrared would be followed at increasingly longer wavelengths by microwaves, which are used for radar, communications and even cooking; and then the radio bands: UHF (ultra high fequency), which is used for television transmission, then VHF (very high frequency), and short, medium and long waves, all familiar from transistor radios (see *Fig. 1*).

'Beyond' visible light at shorter wavelengths in this total spectrum of electromagnetic energy would be first invisible ultraviolet 'light' which is often referred to as 'blacklight' ('ultra' is the Latin for 'beyond'). At still shorter wavelengths the ultraviolet would be followed by the very high energy

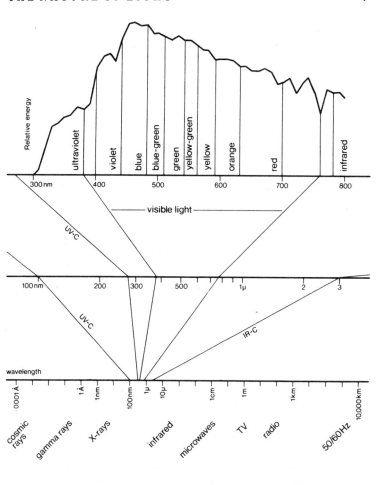

Fig. 1

The spectrum of electromagnetic energy. This shows the energy distribution in daylight at the top (the CIE standard distribution D_{65}) and the way this small range of wavelengths relates to the rest of the electromagnetic spectrum. The two lower scales are logarithmic: each step in the bottom scale is ten times the step before, which allows all these wavelengths to be shown in one diagram.

X rays and gamma rays: it is the exceedingly powerful and penetrating gamma rays which constitute part of the spectre of nuclear radiation.

Two further concepts are closely linked to that of wavelength: frequency and the quantum. The frequency of electromagnetic radiation is simply the rate at which the waves of any given wavelength undulate or vibrate. Frequency is expressed as the number of Hertz (Hz), that is, the number of complete waves a second, after Heinrich Hertz who discovered electromagnetic radiation in 1888. The link between frequency and wavelength derives from the fact that light will always travel the same distance in a second, so that the number of waves during that second is always associated with the distance between each wave. Thus for light of longer wavelengths, there are fewer waves and the frequencies are lower than for light of shorter wavelengths.

The 'photon' is the name given to one quantum of light energy, and a quantum can be thought of as the basic and indivisible unit or particle of electromagnetic radiation. The energy conveyed by light varies with the frequency, and so is different for each wavelength. As the frequency increases the energy carried also increases, so that violet light at a wavelength of 400 nanometres (millionths of a millimetre, abbreviated as nm), which is nearly twice the frequency of red light at 700 nm, is also nearly twice as energetic — 72 kilocalories per mole compared with 44 kilocalories per mole for red light. In this context a 'mole' is a unit of quantity and in the case of light it defines a very large number indeed of photons — 6×10^{23}.

The nature of light itself really does not submit to the

commonsense notions of our everyday world since it behaves both as if it were a continuously vibrating wave and also as if it were a stream of separate particles of energy, apparently depending on how we choose to observe it. Again it is outside the scope of this book to discuss the quantum mechanics of light, but the concept of the photon is important to modern physics and now biology, and thus to a number of the explanations of the effects of light which are discussed in this book.

The primary sunlight which crosses 93 million miles of empty space to reach us is softened and tempered by the atmosphere which acts as a giant gaseous filter. The high-energy, harmful far-ultraviolet is almost completely filtered out by the layer of ozone gas in the upper atmosphere so that less than one percent of the sun's energy reaching the earth's surface has a wavelength shorter than 320 nm, and essentially no radiation shorter than 285 nm penetrates at all. In the infrared, wavelengths of over 900 nm are increasingly absorbed by water vapour in the atmosphere and at longer wavelengths by carbon dioxide. This results in a daylight spectrum (radiation from the whole canopy of sky, whether cloudy or sunny) which remains remarkably steady most of the time. Daylight is largely equal in energy across the band of visible light wavelengths, rising slightly in intensity towards the blue end of the spectrum, and although its intensity begins to fall off steeply in the violet, it does have a significant proportion of invisible near-ultraviolet radiation, particularly when the sun is high in the sky. (Where the term daylight is used in this book it is intended to denote the full range of wavelengths which penetrate the atmoshere, including the invisible ones). Although we cannot see the near-ultraviolet in daylight, this waveband — technically, UV-A (400 nm to 315 nm) and UV-B (315 nm to 280 nm) — which has higher energy than any of the visible wavelengths, turns out to be highly active biologically and plays a crucial role in the way our bodies respond to light.

So light is indeed a form of energy bouncing about in the outside world — since most objects reflect light, just as most also absorb it, only a few letting it pass through unimpeded — but in addition to this, it is apparent that light has effects in the body which run a good deal deeper than these bald facts would appear to suggest.

Sun and Skin

We do not need to look far to find the first evidence that light has an effect on us going beyond our ability to see. It is a commonplace that sunlight falling directly on the skin produces a suntan fairly quickly: and a suntan represents a series of subtle chemical changes which have taken place in our skin in response to the near-ultraviolet in sunlight. Less subtle but equally well known is sunburn or 'ultraviolet erythema', which is usually the result of impatience with the more gradual changes involved in acquiring a suntan. The fact that having a suntan has become such a potent status symbol in the industrialized West is some indication of our concern about the effects of increasingly depriving ourselves of natural daylight.

We already know that this concern is well grounded since, associated with the process of tanning, there is a reaction which forms an essential vitamin in our skin in response to the same invisible portion of the sunlight spectrum, the near-ultraviolet. This is vitamin D or, as it is now more correctly called, calciferol. Another chemical, 7-dehydro-cholesterol, which is freely available in the body, is converted into calciferol in the skin by a reaction which is entirely dependent on energy supplied by the near-ultraviolet in sunlight, and the calciferol is then released into the bloodstream. Calciferol, or vitamin D, is virtually unavailable in any food except fish. A substitute known as vitamin D_2, or ergocalciferol, which is made from a plant extract, is added to milk in America to prevent vitamin D deficiency; but in Britain and other European countries it is barred by the food regulations, because, although small amounts are vital, very large amounts can be poisonous.

Although calciferol is referred to as a vitamin as a result of a historical controversy over its identification, it is now generally accepted that calciferol is actually an essential steroid hormone. The liver and kidneys together act to 'switch on' and regulate calciferol levels in the blood. This, in conjunction with the level of the hormone thyrocalcitonin and the parathyroid hormone, is intimately related to the delicate management of the level of calcium in the blood. Thus in children an absence of calciferol leads to rickets, a calcium deficiency disease of the bones.

In addition to calciferol's control of mineral levels it has other, still obscure, effects which relate to the similarity of its molecular structure to other steroid hormones with which it interacts. This may possibly represent another route for some of the more fundamental physiological effects which are described later.

Races and peoples traditionally living in the tropics have inherited a high level of permanent skin pigmentation as a protection against the continuous high level of near-ultraviolet in tropical daylight which would otherwise lead to the formation of too much calciferol. At higher latitudes, for example in Northern Europe, a minimum of skin pigmentation is needed because in winter, when the sun is low in the sky, ultraviolet levels are also very low and the skin needs to be as sensitive as possible. The gradual seasonal variation in ultraviolet intensity at higher latitudes allows time for a controlled change in the level of skin pigmentation; as summer comes a natural suntan steadily deepens. Sunburn is the painful result of increasing the amount of ultraviolet exposure faster than the skin can adapt to it.

Nevertheless it seems that a lightly pigmented skin cannot adapt enough to protect itself fully against continuous high levels of near-ultraviolet. The shorter ultraviolet wavelengths in sunlight have considerably higher energy than the visible wavelengths. Although they do not penetrate so far into the skin as the longer wavelengths, they are readily absorbed by the 'nucleic acids' such as the famous double helix chemical DNA, which embodies the genetic code in the nucleus of every cell. (Cells are the individual microscopic compartments in animals and plants into which the living matter is organised.) DNA can be damaged by absorbing ultraviolet radiation and although it has the ability to repair itself this repair is never total, so that genetic errors gradually accumulate. The current theory is that as these errors build up, the skin ages prematurely and the chance of skin cancer increases. The fact that this would need both sustained high levels of near-ultraviolet exposure and sensitive skin is borne out by the relative rarity of skin cancer except among fair-skinned people spending their lives in the tropics.

The shining of light on the surface of the skin has come into use as a treatment for various diseases in the past twenty years. Light actually penetrates quite deeply into the body. One study in the early 1960's (Van Brunt et al, 1964) reported measuring light inside the brains of living sheep, and it has been discovered that various internal chemical changes can be brought about spontaneously or induced by shining light on and through the skin.

The most striking example is provided by the treatment of a form of jaundice which occurs in new-born babies. About 15 - 20% of premature babies are born with this condition, known as 'neonatal hyperbilirubinemia'. This is the result of a build-up in the baby's blood of a chemical called bilirubin with which the still immature liver of the baby is unable to cope. Bilirubin is a waste product from the breakdown of haemoglobin from expended red blood cells. If it accumulates in the blood it gives rise to the characteristic symptoms of jaundice. A high level of bilirubin in the blood can cause brain damage in new-born babies and thus constitutes a dangerous condition. Until recently the most common treatment was a potentially hazardous total blood transfusion. In the test tube bilirubin itself is bleached and broken down by exposure to light, and in the late 1950's (Cremer et al, 1958) it was discovered that exposing babies with hyperbilirubinemia to high levels of light would actually reduce the levels of bilirubin circulating in their blood. As a result of this finding and the studies that followed, this form of treatment by light, phototherapy, is now in general hospital use for new-born babies with jaundice.

The treatment of the other group of diseases which respond to phototherapy is carried out by first sensitising the body to light. It has been known for many years that when certain chemicals are either applied to the surface of the skin or swallowed, exposure to light can then cause photo-allergy or phototoxicity which may have an impact through-out the body (see Ellinger, 1957). This kind of special sensi-tivity does sometimes occur naturally, as in metabolic disor-ders such as porphyria in which there is a disturbance in the production of the pigment porphyrin. Recently this prin-ciple of inducing photosensitivity has been succesfully used in the treatment of a number of conditions, particularly herpes, psoriasis and vitiligo. Herpes is a virus disease, pso-riasis a skin disease and vitiligo a skin pigmentation disorder, and all three are traditionally quite difficult to treat effec-tively. A photosensitising chemical, such as a psoralen com-pound, is either given or applied to the patient — who is usually then exposed to a bank of special fluorescent lamps producing the wavelengths that the photosensitising chem-ical absorbs best, generally in the blue or near-ultraviolet range. (In the terminology of the lighting industry 'lamp' refers to bulbs and tubes only, not fixtures, and is used in this sense throughout the book.)

It is clear that we need go no further than common knowledge and established medical practice to discover that light can have a marked effect on the way our internal body chemistry is conducted. As soon as we examine the theo-retical biology of light, or 'photobiology' as it is now called, we find that a general response to light is fundamental to the constitution of both animals and plants.

Light Absorption and Photosynthesis

All organisms from the lowliest bacterium to ourselves show some form of sensitivity to light. The easiest way to see this is in behaviour, since animals and plants move, bend or grow towards — and sometimes away from — the light: responses called 'phototropism' in plants and 'phototaxis' in animals.

Although not as obvious as behaviour, there is one vital photobiological process in plants which is familiar to anyone who did biology at school: photosynthesis. This is a kind of celebrity among biological reactions and underlines the intimate links between light and life, since directly or indirectly it feeds all of us. In simple terms it involves the capture of energy from daylight by chlorophyll (the green pigment that gives most plants their characteristic colour) and the use of this energy to build up complex organic molecules within the plant cells.

For any process such as photosynthesis to occur at all, light energy must first of all be absorbed in a way which allows it to be reliably harnessed by specific chemicals or groups of chemicals in the animal or plant. Such energy absorption is basic to our understanding of photobiological reactions, and is the starting point for photobiologists in describing the response of biological systems to light.

A photon of light is absorbed by an atom or molecule

when the photon directly collides with it. Its energy is then taken up by the electrons — the infinitesimal units of electric charge which orbit the nucleus of the atom. Three things can then happen to this extra energy. It can simply be released again as light, as in fluorescence; or it can cause a change in molecular shape but without altering the identity of the molecule, a 'photo-isomerization' ('isomer' comes from the Greek for 'equal parts' — the properties of an isomer may be different, but its constituent atoms are the same); or it can trigger a chemical reaction between the molecule and another one — a photochemical response.

Atoms and molecules do not indiscriminately absorb all the radiation that falls on them; they absorb certain wavelengths only, depending on their own structure. Some materials absorb very little visible light and are quite transparent, like glass — although it does absorb untraviolet. Molecules which only absorb narrow bands of visible light usually belong to strongly coloured chemicals, since they pass or reflect the remaining visible wavelengths, which give them the highly coloured appearance we then see.

Substances with molecules which have the ability to absorb visible light are called pigments; and the basis of photobiological responses is the absorption of light energy — by pigments or pigment systems. These biological pigments include families of chemicals such as the porphyrins, chlorophylls, carotenoids and flavins, which all have a broadly similar molecular structure.

In the higher forms of life, these molecules are carried by specialized structures within the receiving cell, and these cell structures are also all broadly similar despite a variety of functions. In photosynthesis the pigment primarily responsible for absorbing the light energy is chlorophyll 'a'; and the photoreceptor structure within the plant cell is the chloroplast, a tightly organised structure formed from closely packed miscroscopic plates, called lamellae, only 20 nm apart. The chlorophyll forms monolayers, layers that are only one molecule thick, on the surfaces of the lamellae, which ensures that the chlorophyll is spread over the widest possible surface area for the most efficient energy absorption and transfer. The fine structure of the chloroplast closely resembles the internal structure of retinal cells in the eye as explained in the next chapter.

While the absorption of a photon is a primary event in any photobiological response, there are two quite different ways in which the energy gained is put to use. In one the light is important purely for its energy, and in the other the light energy acts simply as a trigger or signal, as in vision — the total energy absorbed not being related to the often much greater energy which may be expended in the response. Photosynthesis, again, is an example of the first of these two categories. The energy absorbed by the chlorophyll is directly harnessed by a complex biochemical system. Energised electrons are transferred away from the chlorophyll and their energy is taken up by two further photochemical pigment systems. These two systems then produce chemicals with complex molecular structures which store large amounts of energy in the form of special phosphate bonds. These chemicals in turn supply the energy needed to synthesize carbohydrates from carbon dioxide and water in the plant cells, a process on which all animal life ultimately depends.

Vision

Vision is undoubtedly the most obvious photobiological response in animals — so obvious that it may seem odd to actually consider it in these terms. Nevertheless, simple as it is for us, our ability to see is rooted in a sophisticated complex of photobiological reactions; and its importance is emphasised by the frequently made claim that more than 80% of all our sensory information about the world is optical.

Sight has been developed during the course of evolution from a variety of simple photosensory cells. These became localized in areas of the skin surface which during evolution folded inwards to form primitive eyelets or ocelli. In invertebrates (animals with no hard internal skeleton, such as insects and crustacea), there are both ocelli, which are very basic light-sensitive structures, and compound eyes, which are composed of many light-sensitive segments packed close together. The more sophisticated refracting eyes are found in vertebrates (animals which do have a hard internal skeleton, such as reptiles, birds and mammals).

In our refracting eyes there are two pieces of transparent tissue with very accurate optical curvature — the cornea and the lens — and together they act in the same way as a lens assembly in a camera (see *Fig. 2*). The biological lens is soft and is usually held stretched flat, but can be allowed to contract by the action of the muscle that surrounds it and holds it

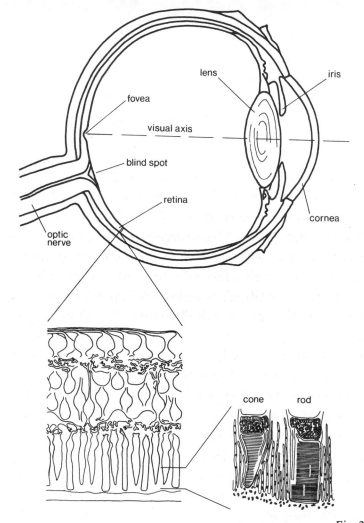

Fig. 2

The structure of the human eye. The expanded cross-section of the retina (lower left) shows the layers of the nerve cells above the rods and cones; the ganglion cells are at the top (feeding nerve fibres away to the left). In this view the light enters the retina from the top: it has to pass through the nerve cell layers to reach the rods and cones. The enlarged view of the rods and cones (lower right) shows the active photoreceptor structures; the many fine layers stacked close together are the lamellae. At this end the rods and cones are embedded in the pigment epithelial cell layer. The numerous small black dots are the pigment granules.

in place. This has the effect of altering its optical curvature and so changing its focus; in a camera with a hard glass or plastic lens it is necessary to move the entire lens assembly backwards and forwards in front of the film. In the eye, instead of light-sensitive film, there are a vast number of light-sensitive living cells which are embedded on the inside of the more or less spherical surface that is the back of the eye. This concave layer of cells is called the retina. Some idea of the fineness of its structure can be gauged from a simple example: when we look at the full moon, the round patch of light which is focused on each of our retinas has an area of only one fiftieth of a square millimetre, the size of a tiny speck of dust, yet this illuminates 700 photoreceptor cells.

The structures inside visual photoreceptor cells are all very similar, both inside the rhabdomere cells of the invertebrates and in the rod and cone cells of the vertebrates. They all employ arrangements of cell membranes which form part of the structure of the receptor cell. These membranes take the form of microtubules in the invertebrates and lamellae in the vertebrates; the lamellae closely resemble the structure of chloroplasts, the plant cell structures that trap and use light energy.

At the chemical level, the process of translating an image focused on the retina into information which can be transmitted to the brain is initiated by pigments in the receptor cells. They absorb the light energy which the cell then converts into nerve impulses.

A single family of pigments has been found in both vertebrate and invertebrate eyes: the carotenoids and the chemicals which are derived from them, such as vitamin A_1 and Vitamin A_2. Thus a derivative of vitamin A, retinal, is bound to a protein called an opsin to form rhodopsin, a common visual pigment. The opsin varies from one species to another and determines the principal wavelengths to which that rhodopsin will respond. When rhodopsins absorb light a photoisomerization (or change in molecular shape) takes place; the energy gained causes a change in shape from what is known as the '11-cis' form of the retinal in the rhodopsin to what is known as the 'all-trans' form. This change of form in turn triggers the transmission of a nerve impulse from the photoreceptor cell. A network of nerves covering the surface of the retina gathers these impulses together and encodes them for transmission out of the back of the eye along the optic nerve.

Most animals have colour vision, which can be defined as the ability to distinguish between different wavelengths of light. It exists in insects, fishes, reptiles, birds and mammals, but the colours seen vary considerably. Vision in moths, for example, is most sensitive at two different wavelengths — in the green, and in the near-ultraviolet (at 360 nm). These two peak responses correspond to the colours of a very faint night-time air glow which we are unable to see.

Our own eyes have two types of visual photoreceptor cells, the rods and the cones. The rods allow us to see at very low light levels — for instance at night — but not in colour; they predominate in the peripheral, off-centre, part of the retina which lets us see 'out of the corner of our eye'. The cones enable us to see in colour in a range between 380 nm in the violet and about 770 nm in the red. They are found throughout the retina but are concentrated principally in a small area at its centre called the fovea, which lies more or less in line with the middle of the lens on the visual axis of the eye. When we move our eyes to look at the world around us, we are constantly bringing the object of our attention into focus on this most sensitive part of the eye. The cone cells contain three different visual pigments which respond to blue, green and red light respectively; it is for this reason that a colour television picture is made up of a mosaic of tiny blue, green and red dots. These three colours are known as the additive primaries — as distinct from the subtractive primaries which are the basis of colour mixing in paints.

We know that the retina can detect light in three broad overlapping bands, but what happens next is only partially understood. There are far more light sensitive retinal cells than there are fibres in the optic nerve; clearly the retina does a lot of 'data processing' on the output from the photoreceptor cells to reduce the information to a manageable volume. In vertebrates the retina is virtually an extension of the brain, comprising hundreds of millions of nerve cells at several different levels of complexity, all with multiple interconnections and interactions. The assumption is that a great deal of the computation needed for colour perception is actually carried out in the retina, and that a coded signal of some kind is despatched along the optic nerve. Opinions vary about the form this coding takes.

In 1957 Leo Hurvich and Dorothea Jameson at the University of New York proposed an 'opponent coding' theory developed from a concept originally put forward by Ewald

Hering in the 1870's (see *fig. 3*). It argues that two different nerve 'channels' carry information about coloured light seen by the retina. Each of these two channels is capable of carrying a varying 'positive' signal or a varying 'negative' signal. Each channel can only carry either a 'positive' or a 'negative' signal at any one time, and this relationship between the competing signals is called 'opponent coding'. The theory holds that one of the two channels signals either red *or* green and that the other signals either yellow *or* blue light, the yellow signal being derived from the output of both red and green photoreceptor cells together.

This theory has been widely adopted since it accounts for many aspects of colour perception including colour blindness and complementary colour effects. In the case of the latter, if there is, for example, an equal stimulus of green and red light in the same place, we do not see a greenish-red — indeed such a colour does not exist — instead we see a neutral grey. The same applies to blue and yellow — again there is no such colour as a yellowish-blue. The opponent coding theory explains that since both these pairs of colours share a single opponent coded channel and since that channel is unable to signal both 'complementary' colours at once, it ends up signalling neither. Of course, colours which involve both opponent coded channels, for instance yellow-green and blue-green, can occur freely and as a result these are familiar colours. The theory can also be applied to the appearance of the rainbow, which does not show the seven distinct bands of colour that Newton implied with his neat designations from red to violet. Instead the small number of uneven bands of merging colours can be largely predicted

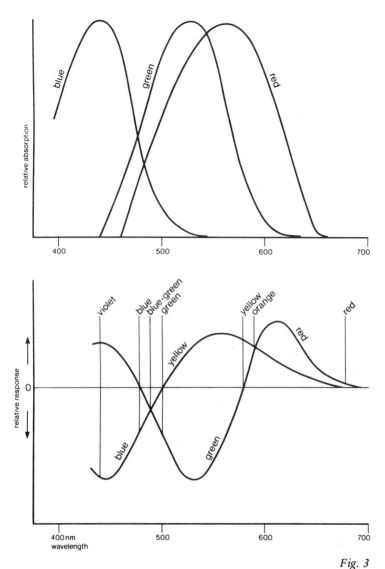

Fig. 3

Colour vision. The top diagram shows the absorption bands of the three different types of cone. The lower diagram illustrates Hurvich and Jameson's 'opponent coding' theory. The two curves are the opponent coding functions, red-green and blue-yellow. Above the neutral axis one colour is signalled, below it the other is signalled. Different colours are seen as a result of the combined responses of the two channels at different wavelengths. For example the best yellow is seen when the red-green channel is at zero, just below 600nm.

from a graph of the two opponent process functions. In addition, a certain amount of physiological evidence suggests that there is indeed this kind of coding in the eyes of some animals.

Nevertheless, opponent coding may only be part of a more complex total scheme preceded, perhaps, by other types of processing. Edwin Land, the founder of the Polaroid Corporation, has made some fascinating observations about the minimum information required to produce the sensation of full colour vision. He has demonstrated that it is possible to generate a fully coloured image using two superimposed black and white transparencies if one of them is both photographed and projected through a filter of a single colour, for example, red. At first hearing, from the standpoint of traditional colour theory this is an astonishing, even unbelievable, result — yet it is easily demonstrated and deserves serious attention. Land has also shown, in carefully devised experiments, that we can still correctly perceive two different colours even when the illumination on each of them is adjusted so that both reflect an *identical mixture* of wavelengths: another equally surprising result.

Land has evolved what he calls the 'retinex' theory (a conflation of 'retina' and 'cortex') to account for these findings. This describes the way in which he believes we are able to maintain the perception of colour as a consistently familiar experience in spite of wide variations in the wavelength distribution and intensity of the illuminating light. We do not, he suggests, perceive the actual intensity of light falling on the three types of cones: our eyes are able to compute the relative reflectance of everything in the field of view very rapidly, regardless of shadows and variations in illumination. They do this by calculating a network of related ratios of brightness on either side of abrupt boundaries, ignoring gradations of brightness between these sharp demarcations. (This is an impressive feat which may be related to the retina's ability to recognise patterns, currently the subject of intensive research.) In this way a 'lightness' value is generated for each well-defined object or area in the whole field of view in each of the three cone pigment bands independently and virtually instantaneously. These 'lightness' values for each object are then brought together and the comparison provides the basic information for our experience of colour. (For a fuller explanation of this theory see Land, 1977.)

It seems that what this boils down to, if Land is right, is that the consistent sensation we call colour, which remains stable even when the 'colour' of the illumination changes, is only possible because vision has a spatial component. If the eye was not capable of deriving information about the location of objects in space, we could not have the particular sensory experience we call colour. Land's black and white slides are actually perceived in full colour because they have enough spatial diversity to supplement their sparse wavelength information and stimulate the mechanism which is responsible for our perception of colour. To turn this round another way, if the eye were to provide an output which did not carry any spatial, that is, visual information, then it would also be unable to compensate for changes in the intensity and spectral distribution of the prevailing light source. This deduction is of considerable pertinence with regard to some of the more controversial findings which are discussed later.

That even these theories do not fully chart the immensely complex retinal processing which permits colour vision is clear from a further snippet of observation. This is a simple and well-known experiment involving a spinning disk, which demonstrates that a rapidly flickering black and white stimulus can produce the sensation of colour depending on its rate of flicker. Doubtless in due time this phenomenon will also find its way into an expanded theory of colour processing in the retina.

Although it is obvious that there is much we have to discover about the precise mechanisms of colour vision, we do know that the colours we see are the result of the retina simply being sensitive to intensity differences in three bands of wavelengths. From this, it is clear that our eyes do not give us a detailed spectral analysis of the *mixture* of wavelengths we are seeing. Instead, not only do we see equal amounts of complementary yellow and blue, or red and green as pale grey, but when all the colours of the rainbow are present together, as in sunlight, we see a pure white light.

Hormones and the Non-Visual Role of the Eye

A new body of evidence is emerging from the shadow of controversy to tell us that the eyes are more than mere cameras for the brain. The eyes of animals (including mammals) and now — we find — of man himself, allow light to play an infinitely more important role in the management of internal chemistry than we have previously suspected. It is slowly being recognised that the whole of the body looks to the eyes for information about the external conditions of light.

In mammals, the signals about light seen by the eyes are carried away from the retina along the optic nerves to the visual cortex at the back of the brain. But there is another, previously disregarded, nerve pathway unconnected with vision running direct from the eye to the part of the brain called the hypothalamus, which controls the pituitary. The pituitary is a small endocrine (that is, hormone producing) gland lying immediately below the hypothalamus in the brain (see *fig. 4*). Little is known about the source of this pathway in the eye, but according to the scientists Thompson (1951) and Becher (1953 and 1955) it starts in the nerve ganglion cell layer of the retina. Becher claims that there is a type of small cell in this nerve layer which is actually a photoreceptor dedicated to providing a non-visual output.

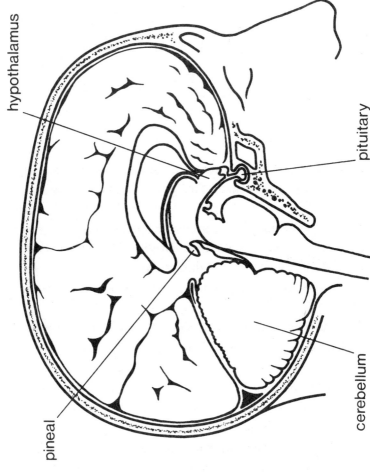

Fig. 4

A section through the human head from front to back showing the position of the hormone glands and parts of the brain discussed in the text. The pituitary occupies a small hollow in the floor of the skull.

The pituitary and the hypothalamus act together to control most of the other endocrine glands in the body. This includes the thyroid, a gland in the neck that controls growth and metabolism, the gonads, which are the sex glands (ovaries and testes), and the adrenals, glands next to the kidneys which release hormones such as cortisone and adrenaline. As a result the hypothalamus is able to control directly, or indirectly through the pituitary, a wide range of functions in the body which are now known to be influenced by the perception of light. These include growth and metabolism, water regulation, temperature regulation, the availability of glucose and other energy 'fuels' in the body, and sexual and reproductive functions (Hollwich, 1979); in short some of the most important processes in the body.

The hypothalamus and the pituitary also control such vital functions as the regulation of appetite, the alternation of sleeping and waking, aspects of behaviour such as fear, rage and sexual drive, and the balance between the two parts of the 'autonomic' nervous system. The autonomic, or involuntary, part of the nervous system acts more or less automatically to co-ordinate the unconsciously regulated activity in the body. Its two parts are the sympathetic, which prepares the body for action and emergency, and the parasympathetic, which is concerned with routine maintenance and restoration of the body's resources.

Light seen by the eye influences the autonomic system by another non-visual route which connects the eye to the pineal, another small endocrine gland in the head. A small number of nerve fibres leaving the eye are diverted along what is known as the inferior accessory optic tract. This allows nerve impulses from the eye to be transmitted out of the brain and down the spinal cord, and we know of at least one pathway this information then takes. Leaving the spinal cord just below the neck at what is called the intermediate thoracic nucleus, it is fed to the superior cervical nerve ganglion of the sympathetic system, which has an output that travels back up to the pineal.

Until the 1960's the function of the pineal body was largely unknown, and even today it is widely ignored, and is usually thought of as an evolutionary vestige without any known function. Yet there has been a discreet reversal of medical opinion, and it is now believed that the pineal may approach in importance the pituitary, long regarded as the 'conductor of the endocrine gland orchestra'. Originally, the pineal was a photoreceptive organ in its own right, and in terms of evolution it predates the eyes at each side of the head, just as the basic light response in animals predates vision (Hollwich, 1979). In lower vertebrates such as the lizard it still functions as a non-visual 'third eye', and in the frog it has cells which show the same structure as those in the frog's retina. In mammals, this direct response to light appears to be obsolete and there are no longer any local nervous connections between the pineal and the surrounding brain. Instead the pineal now receives its input from the sympathetic nervous system, part of it via the pathway from the eye, as described above.

The pineal acts by producing a variety of biochemicals which it releases as a direct response to the arrival of noradrenaline — a substance related to the hormone adrenaline (epinephrine in the U.S.A.). The noradrenaline is secreted by the sympathetic nerve endings at the pineal when nerve impulses arrive along the non-visual route from the eye. Thus the level of activity and secretion in the pineal is determined by the number of sympathetic nerve impulses reaching it; and these impulses are either suppressed or stimulated by the nerve transmission from the eye when the retina responds to light, depending largely on whether the species is active during the day or is nocturnal.

The pineal is described as a 'neuro-endocrine transducer', which is a shorthand way of saying that it translates nerve signals into hormonal messages. Its chief messenger is the hormone melatonin. This is released into both the bloodstream and the cerebrospinal fluid, the shock-absorbing hydraulic cushion which protects and bathes the brain and spinal cord. It has been suggested that melatonin's main site of action is in the brain centres controlling the anterior lobe of the pituitary gland, where it in turn modifies the output of pituitary hormones. Acting in the rest of the body it appears to influence gonadal, adrenal and thyroid functions. In general both the pituitary and the pineal are related in their regulation of the other endocrine glands, the pituitary tending to stimulate and the pineal to inhibit. (For a comprehensive survey of literature on the pineal see Relkin, 1976 and Reiter, 1977.)

In birds and many mammals pineal secretion serves the important function of providing a time signal which synchronizes or entrains the various near-24 hour biochemical rhythms in the body. The level of light in the environment provides the cue for this since the rhythm of pineal secretion is tied to the external cycle of light and dark, which in the natural environment provides a reliable 24 hour timebase. In addition the gradually varying ratio of daylength to night then provides information about the time of year, which is important for seasonal breeding cycles in many mammals. In contrast, studies with people show that while the alternation of light and dark has some influence, it is by no means the only factor involved in the timing of daily biochemical rhythms. (See Hollwich, 1979, pp 25 and 34 - 38.)

Much of the work on these neuroendocrine pathways from the eye has been done in animals and birds, but Fritz Hollwich, who is Professor of Ophthalmology at the University of Muenster in West Germany, has demonstrated that light seen through the eye has a major impact on human internal chemistry as well. In important but little-known studies of people with opaque cataracts in both eyes, examined before and after operations to restore their sight, he has demonstrated that in man internal biochemical bodily functions are remarkably sensitive to light: it has an effect on kidney function and water balance, liver metabolism, thyroid function, the rhythm of cortisol secretion and blood composition including the levels of sex hormones, growth hormones, and the catecholamines (particularly adrenaline and noradrenaline). In each case, Hollwich recorded significant changes — these variables are only normal when adequate light is seen by the eye, and the responses they show are exactly what would be expected if the non-visual pathways already described are active in ourselves as well as in other mammals. The major importance of Hollwich's work has received at least limited recognition: his home state of

North Rhine—Westphalia in West Germany now accepts blood tests which show endocrine and metabolic abnormalities as evidence for the assessment of the extent of occupational disability caused by blindness.

Much more research is needed to uncover the detail which is missing from our present understanding, but it is now safe to conclude that our eyes not only provide a visual output to the brain but also provide a signal for switching and modifying much of the body's hormone production. So it is hardly an exaggeration to assert that light is deeply involved in the biochemical regulation of the entire body, which means that it must also be a vital factor in the maintenance of our health.

Of course we do know that light is essential for human activity, since we need to see, and we provide light for ourselves regardless of its more obscure biological effects. But the importance of colour cannot be side-stepped. We have invented artificial sources of light which can generate a spread or mixture of wavelengths quite unlike daylight in which we know our visual system at least functions best. Research into the effects of different light sources has concentrated on their influence on the visual system — visual acuity, visual fatigue and so on — and the assumption has been made that a light source is satisfactory if it is adequate for seeing by. This assumption will prove wrong if the more controversial evidence which follows is confirmed: for it suggests that our non-visual response is actually more sensitive to colour shifts than our visual system, a conclusion which could oblige the lighting industry to completely re-assess its

criteria for high-quality lighting in order to ask about each
type of light source a new question — is it healthy?

The Response to Colour

The idea that colour has an effect on health goes back as far as the history of medicine itself. Ancient Egyptian medical texts have been found which describe the application of coloured minerals for the relief of various conditions. The Roman physician Celsus, who lived in the first century AD, similarly described coloured plasters to be applied to the skin, including one of a nearly red colour which he considered was effective in making wounds heal more quickly. He also prescribed medicines according to their colour.

Avicenna, the famous Persian physician and philosopher who worked in Baghdad at the beginning of the eleventh century, held colour to be most important in medicine, both for diagnosis and treatment. He believed, for example, that red light stimulated the movement of the blood and that blue light soothed it. So he recommended that people suffering from nosebleeds should avoid looking at anything bright red.

In the Middle Ages in Europe, colour played an important part in medicine: scarlet was used to stop bleeding and as part of the treatment of smallpox. (With such contrary views in their scientific literature on the use of red to staunch blood, one or other protagonist in the crusades should have been at quite an advantage.) In England, King Edward II was prescribed a room entirely in red to counter smallpox.

Also in England, physicians adopted scarlet cloaks as a badge of their profession. Black threads were used to cure earache, and yellow in various forms was used to treat jaundice, understandably since yellow is symptomatic of the illness.

Whether originally rooted in observation, intuition or irrational belief, convictions such as these have persisted. In the 1860's General Pleasonton in Philadelphia made expansive claims for the beneficial effects of blue light and the findings he reported led to a spate of scientific work and considerable public interest. Among other things he maintained that a vine grown in a special greenhouse with one blue pane for every eight clear panes produced two tons of grapes in the third year of growth. Vines not grown in this greenhouse needed five or six years to produce any fruit at all.

During this century, there have been a number of attempts to use colour as a form of therapy or diagnosis in the psychiatric field. In the First World War colours in the form of bright garish patterns were used to treat shell-shock sufferers; the strong colour stimulus seemed to help the recovery of these people invalided by the prolonged intense stress of a battlefield. In 1938 the Worcester State Hospital in Massachusetts reported a series of tests using coloured lights in a mental ward. Red light was found to stimulate depressed patients and blue light had a distinct and sustained quieting effect — this was the most definitive response to the colours they tested.

In 1947 Dr Max Luscher, Professor of Psychology at Basle University, introduced a colour-based personality test which has become well-known and widely used. The test claims to provide accurate psychological information by analysing the order of preference into which the person taking the test spontaneously puts a special range of colours.

That there might be a purely psychological response to colour is perhaps not surprising. But in the field of animal research, where the quest for detailed physiological information is usually initiated, responses to coloured light have also been confirmed, although it is difficult to draw clear-cut conclusions from the results.

During the 1930's Bisonnette reported on the effects of coloured light on starlings, rabbits and goats. Red light stimulated sexual activity and green inhibited it, in contrast with white light, in which activity was normal. In another experiment using red light, Ludwig and Von Ries found that this stimulated growth and weight gain in rats.

In 1940 Kotaru Menju in Japan reported the same results in guinea pigs, with the additional finding that blue light resulted in apparent undernourishment. Also, when the heads and mammary glands of the guinea pigs were illuminated with red light, milk secretion was accelerated, while blue light had the opposite effect: results which Menju attributed to endocrine and autonomic responses. Rabbits under blue light showed an immediate drop in blood pressure, followed later by a pronounced rise; and red light, although showing no immediate effect, later led to a fall in blood pressure. Natumi and Mizutani, in work reported with Menju's, found that blue dye accelerated wound healing, while red dye retarded healing, an effect they attributed to the absorption of red light by the blue dye and absorption of blue light by the red dye. They also reported that red light tended to prevent the growth of tumour tissue while blue light slightly accelerated it.

In 1955 Jacques Benoit and Ivan Assenmacher reported that the growth of the testes of ducklings was greatest in response to green light of 557 nm. But in work reported from 1961 to 1963 Hollwich and Tilgner found that the testes of 5 month old ducklings exposed to red light of 707 nm for 29 days were 16 times larger, and those exposed to orange light of 632 nm were 6 times larger than both those of ducklings exposed to green light of 546 nm and blue light of 436 nm, and than those of control birds. In 1969 Harrison and his colleagues reported that blue and green monochromatic light resulted in the greatest testis development in white leghorn chickens.

The most that can be inferred from these confusing results is that coloured light does seem to have some effect on the gonadal (i.e. sexual) development in some birds, although until the reasons are more completely understood, such results will remain contradictory and present scientists with a continuing challenge.

Nevertheless, for many years coloured lighting has seen limited commercial exploitation in artificially lit enclosures for raising livestock. Chickens are sometimes kept in low intensities of red light, achieved by running incandescent lamps at less than their rated voltage. This is held to produce restful conditions in which the birds gain weight rapidly. Pigs, too, are sometimes kept in dim red light to keep them calm, as blue light apparently encourages fighting and aggression.

These responses however may well be due to reduced light intensity as much as to colour, an explanation which Vriend and Lauber (1973) in Canada have attempted to apply in a more general way to explain such responses to light of different wavelengths.

They put deer mice under red, green and blue light of equal radiant energy and found increased testis weights under the red light. But they also found a similar increase in testis weight in response to increased intensity of white light. Following this result they speculated that the non-visual system might be responding to the number of quanta absorbed regardless of wavelength, so they repeated the experiment using red and blue light only, adjusted to give 'equal photons', and found that the earlier response to red light was absent. Unfortunately they did not include green light in the 'equal photon' part of the study: this might have shown an increase in testis weight over blue and red since the greatest sensitivity and hence the greatest probability of absorbing photons might be expected in the green because the overall spectral sensitivity of rodent eyes peaks in that part of the spectrum. As it is, Vriend and Lauber simply demonstrated that such gonadal responses vary with light energy: using 'equal photons' of red and blue light (because of the much higher quantum energy of blue light), this was tantamount to a reduction of the red radiant energy — which would be expected to reduce the gonadal response given the white light part of their experiment. To be persuasive, their argument would need to be related to an identifiable photo-receptor pigment and rely on only one pigment being active — a condition which might apply in rodents but possibly not in higher mammals which have more sophisticated colour vision.

In view of the inconclusiveness of these studies involving animals it is particularly surprising to discover that there have been a number of studies involving people in which striking and fascinating physiological responses to colour have been demonstrated.

In 1910 Stein showed that there is a change in overall muscle tone in response to light. Tone, in this case, is the continuously maintained but usually moderate contraction of the muscles to maintain body posture. Feré showed that this response varies with colour. Red produced the greatest increase in muscle tone and the effect gradually diminished as the wavelength decreased towards blue. In 1925 Metzger discovered that when light was presented to only one eye the muscular effect was limited to the corresponding side of the body. He also showed that when the side of the face and neck are exposed to blue light, the arms, if stretched out straight in front of the body, will move away from it, but will move towards a similar red light. Ehrenwald found that this response still occurs when the eyes are completely covered, and even in blind people. Hoffman demonstrated too that there are similar responses to both infrared and ultraviolet wavelengths for which we do not have any conscious visual response. These results suggest that another photoreceptor is the skin, which is sensitive to different wavelengths. We have no knowledge of how such a response might occur, although it may perhaps be related in some way to the known sensitivity of nerve cells to light,

(Wolken, 1975) quite possibly involving autonomic nerves.

In 1942 Goldstein reported on work with people suffering from disease of the cerebellum — a part of the brain responsible for muscle tone, balance and the reflex component of voluntary movements. A woman patient of his who had a tendency to fall unexpectedly, and to walk unsteadily, was restored almost to normal when she wore green or blue. When she wore a red dress, her symptoms became more pronounced. Again, this suggests, intriguingly, that the skin can discriminate between different colours.

In 1956 Halpern and Feinmesser reported a range of findings among patients suffering from a one-sided disturbance of balance arising from a variety of causes in the nervous system. These patients displayed a number of disturbed sensory and motor (muscular) functions in response to light of different colours. A typical case was a woman with very severe symptoms involving the right side of her body and the visual field of her right eye. When a red Wratten filter number 24 was put in front of her left eye and her right eye was masked, her whole body immediately began rocking and leaned to the right, while her outstretched right arm moved down and to the right. When a blue Wratten filter number 50 (425 nm) was placed in front of her left eye these effects did not occur at all and she was even better than when there was no filter over her eye. The patient was not even aware of these effects, although she complained of nausea, palpitation (she could feel her heart beating), and difficulty in breathing when looking through the red filter. The pain threshold for a range of loud tones — the volume at which they became painful — was always lowered in these patients when looking through the red filter and always raised when looking through the blue filter. All these responses varied with the amount of blue or red passed by mixed filters, and Halpern reported that opposing effects were produced by two blues when one contained a small amount of red which could not consciously be seen, which indicates that a non-visual response was activated.

After extensive research Robert Gerard, a psychology student at the University of California, Los Angeles, presented a doctoral thesis in 1958 on the psychophysiological responses to light and colour. He used red, blue and white lights evenly diffused across a screen. He monitored blood pressure, the electrical conductivity of the skin, the rate of breathing and heartbeat, the activation of muscles, the frequency of eye-blinking and the EEG (which is the measurement of minute and rhythmically varying electrical voltages produced by the brain − what could be called brainwaves − using a device called an electroencephalograph that picks up signals from the surface of the scalp). Subjective reactions were also recorded. Gerard's findings − based on work with people in good health − confirmed the general proposition that red light is an arousing stimulus while blue light is a calming or sedative stimulus. He found this to be true both subjectively and physiologically. Blood pressure increased under red light and decreased under blue light. Skin conductivity, indicating the arousal of the autonomic nervous system, remained higher under red light than under blue light. The rate of breathing similarly increased under red light, whereas it decreased in blue light. Subjectively, blue light was linked with feelings of calmness and well-being, and red with excitement and tension.

Since the early 1960's a field of investigation which is described as 'applied kinesiology' has been steadily gaining enthusiasts in America. At its simplest, it involves measuring the transient changes in general muscle strength which almost instantaneously follow exposure to a surprising variety of stimuli, including the spectral composition of light. Looking at a large field of colour in daylight immediately reduces muscle strength. The effect is most marked at the red end of the spectrum and least apparent at the blue end. Wearing a coloured garment produces the same effect when the eyes are closed. White, however, does not reduce muscle strength. When particular musical tones (approximately an octave above middle C) are heard at the same time as the coloured field is seen, the colour no longer has the same effect on muscle strength. Following these findings it has also been demonstrated that most ordinary sunglasses, with the exception of grey 'neutral density' ultraviolet transmitting lenses, produce a similar loss of muscle strength, so that in this case the response seems to be to a lack, not of blue light, but of near-ultraviolet (Ott, 1978). Parallels can be found in studies of the improvement in the capacity for muscular work following exposure to ultraviolet; in 1957, for example, Ellinger reported that work output measured on a bicycle ergometer in a laboratory showed an increase of 60% after ultraviolet exposure, a result he attributed to 'decreased fatigability and increased efficiency' (see also Lehmann and Szakall, 1932; Ronge, 1948; Klein and Weis, 1953; and Seidl, 1969). Such changes in muscle performance may be mediated by the autonomic nervous system, although we do not yet know the full extent to which it is influenced by light.

It is surprising that there should be an interaction between things heard and things seen, but this is not a new discovery. In 1931 Zietz reported that low-pitched tones tended to shift the apparent hue of small rapidly-presented patches of colour towards a related darker colour, while high-pitched tones shifted the perceived hue towards a lighter colour. High-pitched tones also had the effect of sharpening after-images — the lingering impression of what has just been seen after the eyes are turned away or closed — while low-pitched tones blurred their outlines. In 1935 Kravkov reported that sound generally decreased the sensitivity of peripheral vision while increasing foveal sensitivity to green and blue, and decreasing foveal sensitivity to red and orange. Later, using minute electric currents in the eye, he found similar effects which could be reversed when the current was reversed. In 1940 Allen and Schwartz in Canada reported that the effects of sound were compensated, after a three minute rest period, by a complete reversal of sensitivity, the red appearing brighter and the green dimmer.

Our thinking, too, may be influenced by what we see. In 1942 Goldstein reported that mental judgements can be influenced by colour. He found that time, size and weight tend to be overestimated in red light and underestimated in blue light. This kind of interplay between different senses and the links between sound and vision could well be the result of an interaction in the brain during the processing of these sensations. In 1968 Herbst reported that concentration even on non-visual tasks, such as memorizing, or the verbal repetition of a spoken statement, improves as light intensity is increased — an intriguing finding. It is also well established that light usually suppresses the alpha wave EEG (a band of 'brain waves' between 8Hz and 13Hz). So other alterations in brain function would not be surprising, particularly since vision commands an enormous amount of processing capacity in the brain, and since we do know that light affects the performance of a key area in the brain, the hypothalamus.

In all this work on the response to colour there is a recurrent observation that red and blue light have effects which parallel the action of the sympathetic and parasympathetic divisions of the autonomic nervous system. This idea was developed as a persuasive hypothesis at least as far back as the early 1960's: Thorne Shipley at the University of Miami, for example, has discussed it at length in an interesting and speculative paper (1964), quoting a wide range of sources in support. The proposal is simple: red stimulates, it increases blood pressure and skin conductivity, and causes a departure from normal muscle tone − all responses which are typical of the action of the sympathetic nervous system and the secretion of noradrenaline; on the other hand, blue sedates, it is associated with a fall in blood pressure and skin conductivity and the maintenance of normal muscle tone (this is the common element in the work of Feré and the kinesiologists), which are typical responses to the action of the parasympathetic nervous system and the secretion of acetylcholine. The sympathetic and parasympathetic parts of the autonomic system work largely in opposition to each other and the hypothalamus can determine which one of the two dominates or is most active at any given time.

It is possible, then, that the balance between red and

blue light seen by the eye is linked to the balance between sympathetic and parasympathetic tone by the action of the hypothalamus. If this is true, it presumably means that the non-visual nerve pathway from the eye to the hypothalamus does carry information about *colour* seen by the eye, and, on Halpern's evidence, is actually more sensitive to the mixture of wavelengths seen than is the visual system.

If corroborated, this conclusion is fundamental, and our next step must be to determine whether the non-visual system is as sensitive to small shifts of colour in white light as it apparently is to such shifts in coloured light, and, if it is, whether long term exposure to light which puts stress on autonomic and endocrine function is detrimental to health and fitness. The overwhelming practical significance of these questions is really the point of this book, but to look for answers we have to turn to evidence which is still profoundly controversial. Evidence which, on its own, clearly needs to be treated with circumspection, but, taken in the context of all the material presented so far, is not only fascinating but compels attention.

'White' Light and Daylight

In 1970 the Kline Chincilla Research Foundation in Illinois announced that, after a five year study, it had been established that using ordinary incandescent light in chincilla breeding rooms (chinchillas are rodents, originally from South America, which are farmed for their fur) resulted in litters averaging 60 - 75% males; but that using 'daylight' clear blue tinted incandescent bulbs reversed this bias, the litters then averaging 60 - 75% females.

The conventional understanding is that sex in mammals is determined entirely by the pairing of sex chromosomes at conception, but apparently sex differentiation remains malleable for a while even after conception (Gluckmann 1978). (Chromosomes are the structures in the cell nucleus into which the gene carrying DNA is organised). Normally individuals with XX chromosomes are female and those with XY chromosomes are male, but these chromosomes merely initiate the process of sex differentiation, they do not fully govern it. The Y chromosome is responsible for the production of androgens (male sex hormones) in the embryo, but this is followed by a succession of developmental steps, primarily the sexual differentiation of the hypothalamus and hence its production of neurohormones, during which sex determination is sensitive to outside factors such as light, noise, temperature and the availability of food. Some of

these factors are capable of causing the hormonal constitution to override the original genetic, or chromosomal,
constitution. So it may be, in the case of these rodents, that
the small colour difference between the two types of 'white'
incandescent bulbs is enough to influence hypothalamic differentiation in half the embryos of each sex. Even if a more
prosaic explanation is adopted, that half the embryos of
one sex or the other are resorbed during gestation (resorp-
tion in the womb does occur in rodents), we are still faced
with a very marked response to what has previously been
considered only a trifling change of colour. One could
quote the adage 'blue for a boy, pink for a girl' if the
polarity of this effect were not exactly the opposite.

The polarity is not, however, always inverted. John Ott,
whose work led to the chinchilla study in Illinois, observed
the effect of sex determination by light first in pumpkins
and then in guppies. In the case of the guppies, which are
popular aquarium fish in America, pink light resulted in at
least 80% females, the remaining males showing significantly
retarded secondary sexual characteristics. Finding such
results in lower vertebrates is, of course, less surprising — it
is known, for example, that if tadpoles are kept at raised
temperatures they all develop into female frogs.

What is surprising is that John Ott is not a scientist but a
professional time-lapse photographer. In spite of this he will
probably be remembered not for the film he has taken, but
for his almost incidental discoveries about the responses in
plants and animals to what were previously considered marginal and insignificant variations in the spectral balance of

artificial lighting. The eye, or rather our visual system, is very tolerant about what it will accept as white: as long as light has a roughly equal proportion of all invisible wavelengths, individual wavelengths or small bands of wavelengths can vary considerably in intensity and the light will still be seen as white. This is exactly what happens with artificial light sources.

Ott's initial observations came about by chance: simply changing one type of ordinary 'white' fluorescent tube for another was enough, he found, to produce quite unexpected changes in the plants he was patiently filming over weeks or even months as they slowly unfolded, a process which was later condensed into only a few moments of screen time. The technique of time-lapse filming is to take one frame at a time at intervals ranging from a few seconds to several hours, or even longer, and then to run the resulting film through a projector at normal speed — usually 24 frames a second — so that the original event is vastly speeded up. The fortuitous combination of using artificial light with time-lapse photography enabled Ott to reveal subtle long-term changes which in many cases might have remained unnoticed at their natural speed. He began to investigate the responses he found, sometimes simply to be able to complete a time-lapse project, often out of curiosity, and gradually came to the conclusion that any departure from the daylight spectrum in lighting leads in the long run to impaired health and behavioural difficulties. Although he was initially only working with plants, he later found that this applied to animals and even people, and that the effects are greater and occur more quickly the more the lighting differs from daylight.

Most of Ott's work has been presented in the form of two popular books (1958 and 1973). Among the few formal papers he has written, one (1964a), although involving only a single type of mammalian cell, closely mirrors his general findings. Asked to undertake a programme of time-lapse cine-micrography (filming through a microscope) to determine the effect of various drugs on living cultures of pigment epithelial cells from rabbit retinas, Ott found that the cells in fact responded much more vigorously to coloured light produced by the filters on the phase contrast microscope he was using. This was a complete surprise, since these cells, although part of the retina, are not known to have any visual or photoreceptive function. Exposing the cells to blue light, he records, caused abnormal pseudopodial activity (pseudopodia are temporary protrusions of the cell wall), while red light actually caused the cell walls to rupture, allowing the cytoplasm to run out (cytoplasm is the semi-liquid part of the cell contents): such rupture amounts to death for a cell. Ott, of course, is not the only person to have observed cellular responses to strongly coloured light, and it is probable that at least some of the mechanisms responsible for these effects have already been encountered in the extensive work at the biochemical and cellular level. A case in point would be the known inhibition of tissue respiration by blue light (Ninnemann et al, 1970; Epel, 1973) which occurs because blue light is absorbed by cytochrome oxidase in the mitochondria (the high-energy-phosphate-producing 'power plants' of the cell).

Ott went further. In fresh preparation of cells, time-lapse filming revealed that the pigment granules, after which the pigment epithelial cells are named, circulated actively throughout the entire cell. After being exposed for 12 hours a day for one week to ordinary incandescent light, an estimated 90% of the pigment granules had become sluggish in their circulation and tended to remain stationary at one end of the cell. However, when a very low intensity of near-ultraviolet was added to the light from the incandescent lamp, all the pigment granules became active again and moved in their original pattern within the cell. The response of chloroplasts in the cells of a grass called elodea proved to be almost identical. Here the natural streaming of the chloroplasts round the cell in unfiltered sunlight, as revealed by time-lapse, was interrupted by putting a piece of ordinary window glass in the light path. Since ordinary glass blocks ultraviolet, the loss of near-ultraviolet was presumed to be responsible. Ott also discovered that mitosis (cell division for growth) would not occur in cells which had been exposed to either red or blue light for more than about twelve hours, but only under a fuller spectrum of white light.

The benefits of near-ultraviolet seemed to depend crucially on its low intensity in a stronger source of white light. When Ott increased the intensity of ultraviolet in illumination of pigment epithelial cells beyond the proportion found in daylight, the cells responded abnormally and died within two hours. That only a certain relative level or proportion of near-ultraviolet gave beneficial results should not be surprising: it can be compared directly with our need for a certain percentage of oxygen in the air we breathe. If there were too much the air would be toxic, and too little would starve us of energy.

Similar responses were discovered in plants and in 'intact' animals. Using the C_3H breed of laboratory mice, a strain so inbred that the mice develop tumours spontaneously and die after a number of months of life, Ott showed that the length of time before this spontaneous tumour formation varied considerably with the type of light under which the mice were kept. Mice under various types of fluorescent light developed tumours and died up to twice as soon as others kept outside under ultraviolet transmitting plastic or an air curtain (Ott arranged the 'air curtain' by venting air from the laboratory out through an open-air cage fitted with a mesh screen to exclude insects). The mice kept under pink fluorescent light fared worst, showing very marked adverse reactions including the withering and loss of their tails, calcium deposits in the heart tissues, smaller numbers in litters and behavioural problems. Mice kept under dark blue fluorescent lamps had more cholesterol in their blood than those kept under red fluorescent light. The males under blue light also became obese; the females did not. Ott noticed that when mice were bred in daylight under an air curtain or ultraviolet transmitting glazing, the males could safely be left with the litters, although it is usual to remove them because they tend to eat the newborn. More than 2000 mice were involved in this experiment, but Ott has only reported the data in general descriptive terms, never publishing a full presentation and analysis of the results. Nevertheless, from the few details he has documented, it is interesting to note that while the survival rate of these mice was most improved (from 61% to 94%) as the balance of visible light approached that of daylight, in contrast the number of months of life before death from spontaneous tumour development increased most (9.4 weeks to 15.6 weeks) not through improvements in the visible spectrum, but through a simple changeover from natural daylight filtered by glass to daylight filtered only by near-ultraviolet transmitting plastic (Ott, 1965). This suggests that there are at least two different modes of response underlying the results he obtained.

Support from a handful of conventional researchers has been gained for Ott's early work. In 1960 and 1961 Samuel Gabby at the Sherman Hospital in Illinois had carried out an initial study for Ott using C_3H mice. He kept thirty pairs of these mice under daylight white fluorescent light, thirty under pink fluorescent and eight as controls behind window glass in daylight. Under pink fluorescent light the mice developed cancer three months earlier, and under the daylight white tubes two months earlier than the control group in daylight. The numbers in litters were also affected; under pink light there were only one or two mice in each litter, whereas under daylight white tubes and daylight there were between six and fifteen in each litter (Wright et al, 1969). Again, there is an indication of two different components in the response.

Rats given carcinogens ('carcinogen' is the Greek for 'cancer causing') were studied by Katherine Sydnor at the Ben May Laboratory for Cancer Research, and she reported informally to Ott in 1961 that rats kept in total darkness showed significantly less tumour development than similar rats kept under daylight white fluorescent lamps which in turn developed less cancer than rats kept under ordinary incandescent lamps.

In 1963 Edward Scanlon at the Evanston Hospital in Chicago compared the lifetimes of hamsters with transplanted tumours under cool white fluorescent light at the hospital and in natural daylight under the air curtain at Ott's laboratory. Hamsters with a fast-acting tumour implant showed little difference in lifespan, but those with a slower-acting type of tumour lived on average for 43 days under the air curtain, but for only 29 days under the cool white fluorescent lamps.

Since this work in the early 1960's these general findings have been confirmed by other researchers. They include Richard Wurtman and Jeffrey Weisel at MIT (the Massachusetts Institute of Technology), and Theodore Sery at the Wills Eye Hospital (their work is described later). Cora Saltarelli at the Roswell Park Memorial Institute in Buffalo also reported in 1976 that the blood chemistry and organ weights of Ha/ICR mice differed under various colours of fluorescent light.

At the very least, Ott's corroborated findings demonstrate that the lighting in animal laboratories where, for instance, drugs and chemicals are tested should be taken into account in the conclusions we reach and apply to ourselves. But at its most controversial, Ott's work involves almost identical responses in people.

In the summer of 1959 the Bellevue Medical Center in New York was persuaded by Ott to run a pilot study in which fifteen cancer patients were asked to spend as much time as possible under natural daylight without their glasses, especially sunglasses, and to avoid sources of artificial light, including television. Ott's insistence on the removal of glasses sprang from his growing conviction that some of the physiological effects of light are mediated directly by the eye. At the end of the summer, fourteen of the patients showed no further advance in their cancer and some showed possible improvement; the fifteenth had not fully understood the instructions but had continued wearing ordinary glasses which block most of the ultraviolet in sunlight — thus serving inadvertently as a partial but revealing experimental control.

This suggestion of an involvement with cancer processes is actually not unreasonable. In a major summary of work on the pineal published in 1976, Richard Relkin at the Easton Hospital in Pennsylvania concluded that the pineal gland does have the ability to check the growth and spread of cancer tissue. We know that the pineal responds indirectly to light seen by the eye, and also that responses to the spectral balance of light are widespread in the body, so it is only a short step to speculate that the extent to which the pineal is able to exert this restraining influence is related in some way to the spectral balance of the prevailing lighting. Certainly at the cellular level light is able to induce sufficiently fundamental changes to make an influence on cancer development quite feasible. And it is interesting that the effects of blue light on pigment epithelial cells photographed by John Ott are reminiscent of the effects of viral attack, which may be linked with some types of cancer. Far from being yet another cancer 'scare', this possibility of light helping to alleviate cancer clearly deserves further investigation. But it needs to be distinguished from recent press reports of studies in which fluorescent lamps actually caused cancer in mice. In these studies cell damage was induced in cultures of mouse tissue exposed within inches of fluorescent tubes, followed by injection of these cells into mice; an artificial procedure quite unlike the spontaneous reactions being discussed, although it is interesting that such cell damage is less severe when the light output of the fluorescent tube more closely approximates daylight (Jacobson et al, 1978; also Bradley and Sharkey, 1977 and Kennedy et al, 1980).

In pointing to the need for near-ultraviolet in lighting, Ott is in good company. Since the 1920's there has been work suggesting that the number of colds among factory workers could be reduced (Maughan and Smiley, 1929; Gage, 1930; Sherman, 1938; Allen and Cureton, 1945; Ronge, 1948), and that physical fitness and the capacity for muscular exertion could be improved (Lehmann and Szakall, 1932; Allen and Cureton, 1945; Ronge, 1948; Klein and Weis, 1953, Ellinger, 1957; Seidl, 1969) by low-level exposure to ultraviolet. In 1954 William Rowan, a photobiologist known for his work on the response to seasonal changes in day-length, suggested at the First International Photobiological Congress that the populations of certain arctic birds and mammals follow a ten year cycle in the intensity of ultraviolet in polar daylight, peaking when the ultraviolet is at its greatest.

In Russia there has been a considerable amount of work demonstrating the benefits of small amounts of ultraviolet in interior lighting. In 1966, Zamkova and Krivitskaya at the Pedagogical Institute in Leningrad reported on the use of ultraviolet in school classrooms with 13 and 14 year old children, concluding that reaction times, working ability and resistance to fatigue were all improved. The children in the experimental group also gained more weight and grew faster than the control group. In 1967 Volkova reported that catarrhal infections and colds were reduced and indicators of resistance to disease showed improvement when ultraviolet was added to the lighting of a machine shop. Also in 1967 Dantzig, Lazarev and Sokolov presented a paper to a meeting of the Commission Internationale de l'Eclairage (CIE) in Washington, explaining the benefits of long-wave ultraviolet which had been observed over several years, first in animals and then in various groups of the Soviet population. This led to standards being set for daily ultraviolet exposure for workers in environments lacking natural light, such as mines and windowless factories. The researchers also explained that these prescribed levels were defined provisionally in terms of a fraction, usually half, of the minimum daily dose that would cause an untanned skin to be just noticeably reddened. This 'minimum erythemal dose' is a way of specifying the daily exposure in terms of its cumulative biological effect rather than simply recommending a particular radiant power level. There have also been a number of Russian papers reporting the effectiveness of ultraviolet in the treatment and prevention of conditions ranging from rheumatism to cerebral atherosclerosis — hardening and thickening of the walls of arteries in the brain (Karacevceva, 1971; Zilov, 1971; Kunitsyna, Yezhova, Cerfus, Pertsovskiy and Sarzhisko, 1977; Pertsovskiy and Kunitsyna, 1977).

Some of the benefits derived from near-ultraviolet will

undoubtedly be due to increased vitamin D formation in the skin, but there are hints both of alternative receptor sites and of alternative channels or modes of influence. The studies of short-term changes in muscle performance by Hoffman and Ellinger suggest a faster-acting response than vitamin formation. Ott's work with pigment epithelial cells from rabbit retinas demonstrated that there is at least one type of ultraviolet responsive cell in the eye, even though this may be incidental to the photo-responsive function of the eye. In 1969 Philip Salvatori, Chairman of Obrig Laboratories in Florida, demonstrated that the iris of the human eye reacts to ultraviolet in spite of the lack of any visual response at these wavelengths. He fitted a patient with a clear ultraviolet transmitting contact lens in one eye and a transparent but ultraviolet blocking one (i.e. a standard clear contact lens) in the other. In artificial light without any ultraviolet the size of both pupils was the same, but in sunlight the iris of the eye covered with the ultraviolet transmitting lens closed appreciably more than the iris of the ultraviolet screened eye. Although the iris itself may have some direct response to ultraviolet, it is quite possible that this effect is mediated by the retina, since the refractive part of the eye is transparent to ultraviolet down to 290 nm (Kinsey, 1948) which coincides with the ultraviolet transparency of the atmosphere; and the iris response is controlled by the autonomic nervous system along a non-visual nerve pathway from the eye. Salvatori's findings also suggest that most ordinary sunglasses may defeat their own object by deliberately blocking near-ultraviolet as most of them do, thus hampering the eye's own protective mechanism, quite apart from the adverse effect they are having on our health.

Ott's claims about the adverse long-term effects of even slight departures from the daylight spectrum, not only in the near ultraviolet but also in the visible, have not been welcomed with much enthusiasm by the scientific community or the lighting industry. This can be traced in part to a difference between Ott's practical perspective and the strictly analytical line followed in much conventional experimental work involving coloured light. Ott has argued that in studying complex intact organisms, it is an error to regard any abnormal response elicited by a narrow colour band as the positive action of those wavelengths. The normal natural response appears to occur under the full spectrum of raw daylight, so it is more logical to attribute any response under particular colours or wavelengths to the relative absence or deficiency of some other wavelengths normally present in daylight, which thus becomes the model lighting spectrum. As a convenient way of expressing this concept, Ott refers to the photobiologically effective range and balance of wavelengths found in daylight as 'full-spectrum' light. This approach is straightforward to explain, but technically it is considerably more difficult to engineer an experiment which examines the effect of 'full-spectrum' light with a particular waveband missing than it is to observe the effects of a more easily generated single band or colour of light.

Nevertheless Ott's work has provoked considerable interest. In 1967 a fluorescent lamp manufacturer in New Jersey introduced a new type of fluorescent tube which was specifically designed to take advantage of the probable benefits of 'full-spectrum' light. It gives an approximation to natural daylight including the near-ultraviolet, and numerous reports have now confirmed that benefits are offered by this tube and its predecessor, which was similar but lacked the near-ultraviolet spectral component.

These tubes made it possible to keep certain snakes and lizards alive in zoo collections for the first time. For example, Josef Laszlo at the Houston Zoo in Texas reported in 1969 that a specimen of snake called *Trimeresurus purpureomaculatus* had refused all food in the six months since it had arrived at the zoo and was of a type notoriously difficult to keep healthy in captivity; nevertheless it started eating again after twelve days exposure to the full-spectrum fluorescent light.

A study of calcium absorption in elderly male residents of the Chelsea Massachusetts Soldiers Home was made in 1971 by Robert Neer of the Massachusetts General Hospital in Boston. In experiments during the winter of 1968 and the spring of 1969 he found that the absorption of calcium from the diet of these men was significantly improved by exposure to the new full-spectrum tubes in comparison with cool white fluorescent lamps. This finding is of some potential importance since in elderly people osteoporosis is common, and this condition, which results in brittle bones, is likely to be relieved by anything which improves calcium uptake or metabolism.

In 1969 Richard Wurtman and Jeffrey Weisel at MIT reported that rats born and reared under these lamps showed different organ weights at fifty days in comparison with similar animals kept under cool white fluorescent tubes. The testes, ovaries and hearts of the rats kept under full-spectrum light were significantly larger than those of rats kept under cool white lamps. Their spleens, however, were significantly smaller, which has been attributed by one commentator to the possible long-term effect of increased physiological stress in the animals kept under cool white fluorescent lamps.

Theodore Sery and two colleagues at the Wills Eye Hospital in Philadelphia reported in 1973 that they had found it less easy to induce tumour development in BALB/c albino mice (another inbred strain) under full-spectrum lights than under pink, warm white, or cool white tubes.

In an experiment at a school in Sarasota in Florida, six year old children in windowless classrooms with full-spectrum tubes in fluorescent fixtures shielded to prevent any stray non-light radiation (this is discussed later) showed a significant decrease in hyperactive behaviour and improved academic achievement compared with pupils in rooms with standard cool white fluorescent lighting and no additional screening. This was part of a two year study carried out by Lewis Mayron with the Nuclear Research Programme at the Veterans Administration Hospital at Hines in Illinois, undertaken with Ott, Amontree and Nations between 1974 and 1975. Dental decay in the experimental group was substantially lower, an effect which has also been reported in hamsters by Sharon at the School of Dentistry at the University of the Pacific in San Francisco, and Feller and Burney in Boston in 1970; and in the cotton rat by Feller, Edmonds,

Shannon and Madsen in Houston in 1974. This reduced dental decay may be the result of altered calcium metabolism through increased calciferol formation, but this is not clear-cut, since in Feller's study incandescent and full-spectrum light both showed a lower incidence of decay (dental caries) than cool white fluorescent. Alternatively there may be some other endocrine influence, or changes in the flow or composition of saliva. In fact Feller both quotes work from the 1940's and the mid 1960's suggesting that dental caries in humans is inversely related to exposure to sunlight (more sunlight means less decay), and also refers to work two and three years earlier by Shannon suggesting that there may be changes in the composition of saliva when illumination is changed.

Better visual acuity and less physiological fatigue in a group of students after four hours studying under full-spectrum fluorescent lighting as compared with cool white were demonstrated in 1974 by Maas, Jayson and Kleiber at Cornell University.

In Florida a manufacturer of contact lenses designed a complete new building with full-spectrum lighting and full spectrum glazing, using ultraviolet transmitting plastic instead of window glass. They reported a noticeable improvement in the morale of employees and an estimated 25% increase in production; moreover, during a severe nationwide epidemic of Hong Kong 'flu in the winter of 1968 - 1969 not a single employee in the total workforce of one hundred fell ill, although statistics for the rest of Sarasota county showed that as many as five percent of the population simultaneously had influenza at that time (Ott, 1973).

The hormone balance of the body seems to be specifically affected by different types of artificial light. In Germany in 1977 Fritz Hollwich reported the effects of cool white fluorescent light, full-spectrum and natural light on the levels of the hormones ACTH and cortisol in the blood of a group of students. ACTH (adreno-cortico-tropic hormone) is a pituitary hormone which stimulates production of cortisol in the outer cortex of the adrenal glands, while cortisol increases the release of glucose into the blood from its storage form, glycogen. When the body is under stress, either from physical injury or as signalled by raised adrenaline levels, increased amounts of cortisol are produced to counter the adverse effects. Hollwich found that exposure for two weeks to cool white fluorescent light at 3500 lux (fairly bright light) resulted in a continual rise in ACTH and cortisol, reaching 'stress levels'. (The 'lux' is a unit of light intensity used by lighting engineers. Recommended levels for interior lighting range from about 500 lux to about 5000 lux). Within two weeks of returning to natural daylight the ACTH and cortisol had recovered to their normal levels. In contrast 3500 lux of full-spectrum light under the same conditions produced a significantly less pronounced reaction of ACTH and cortisol secretion, indicating that the full-spectrum light is tolerated rather better in terms of the response of our endocrine system, and by implication, of the chemistry of the rest of the body (Hollwich, 1979).

In 1979 Greiter, Guttman and Bachi reported on a three year study in Austria showing that regular exposure to both natural daylight and full-spectrum artificial light led to significant improvements in the capacity for physical work and oxygen uptake, and reduced heart rates in the students studied. Similar benefits were also found after exposure to 'full-spectrum' light without the near-ultraviolet component.

This evidence is reinforced by favourable informal reports from a number of countries where these tubes have been installed — in England, for example, they are in use in a handful of hospitals; with great success as a light for plants and even in experimental work involving multiple sclerosis sufferers.

The case Ott has advanced is becoming persuasive. It does seem that we should not presume that our non-visual response to light will turn out to have the same characteristics as our vision. One attribute our visual system has is its ability to decipher the true reflectivity of objects in the field of view regardless of quite considerable changes in the intensity and spectral balance of the illuminating light, and at first glance it seems fair to assume that any non-visual system deriving information from the retina will share this attribute so that any light source adequate for vision will also be adequate for our non-visual requirements. But, as Becher has suggested, the non-visual system may have its own special photoreceptors; and it would perhaps also be surprising if the sophisticated spatial arithmetic presumably needed to enable us to experience colour were applied to a much more basic task which phylogenetically — that is, in terms of evolution — also predates the visual system. Without the kind of spatial calculations which Land has described, any output from the eye which is derived from more than one type of photoreceptor would faithfully report even minor changes in the spectral balance of the prevailing light source, or changes in its intensity.

The thrust of the work reported here is that the non-visual system is indeed sensitive to spectral balance in a way that the visual system is not. Similarly many of the physiological responses to light show a relationship to its real intensity: Herbst reported that mental concentration improves with light intensity; and Hollwich has demonstrated, for example, that the numbers of eosinophil white cells in the blood fall increasingly as the light intensity rises (the eosinophil count falls during active daylight hours), a response which only begins to level off at 20,000 lux, many times brighter than we require for full colour vision. In contrast, the visual system strives to maintain the same subjective impression regardless of the light level. So far there is no evidence that the body has any means of protection against unnatural spectral balance in environmental lighting, presumably because such conditions are not encountered in nature. Instead, it seems that any wavelength imbalance is faithfully relayed by the non-visual system and, through the impact this has on autonomic and endocrine function, many, perhaps most, physiological processes in the body are impaired. Inevitably this shows as a generalized tendency to ill-health — marginal ill-health over the long term, perhaps, but when this might involve working ability, dental decay, heart disease or cancer, some action does need to be taken.

So, if we provisionally adopt the conclusion that light has to confirm to certain criteria — probably those of daylight — if it is to be physiologically benign, we are faced with a simple, practical question: What immediate steps can we take to provide our homes and places of work with 'full-spectrum' light?

Natural and Artificial Lighting

There are fundamentally only two ways of lighting the interiors of buildings: the first is simply to make a hole in the wall, a traditional method discovered early in the practice of architecture; and the second is to have a source of light inside the building. In the first case people want to cover the hole with something transparent and the problem is to find a hard sheet material which approaches the transparency of air; and in the second case it is not easy to devise sources of artificial light which are cheap and bright, and also white enough. In many cases there are drawbacks and side-effects which need to be carefully balanced against the advantages gained.

Since daylight is the model source of light, the easiest way to provide full-spectrum interior lighting is to use windows which let daylight in. But this is not as straightforward as it sounds. Ordinary glass, although it transmits well in the visible portion of the spectrum and fairly well in the infrared, blocks ultraviolet, which it cuts off sharply around 360 nm (*see Fig. 5*). It is technically possible to make glass which transmits ultraviolet: from 1926 to 1939 a glass company in Lancashire in England manufactured a glass which transmitted approximately 50% of the wavelengths in the range 295 nm to 315 nm, but apparently it was not a commercial success and was discontinued at the outbreak of the Second

World War (Copley, 1979). The principal 'full-spectrum' alternative to glass at present is an ultraviolet transmitting form of acrylic sheet, a clear plastic which is sold under a variety of trade names. In fact pure acrylic transmits well up to the atmospheric cut-off point around 300 nm, but it is usually manufactured with an additive specifically intended to block ultraviolet. This is because a great deal of acrylic sheet has been used for aircraft glazing, for which ultraviolet screening at high altitude is essential, and ultraviolet transmission has not been important for other uses. Nevertheless one or two large plastics companies in America and Europe make acrylic in a special ultraviolet transmitting grade, which in America has been shown to withstand outdoor exposure to strong sunlight for many years without deterioration. Its one major disadvantage in comparison with glass, which has a hard surface, is that acrylic is comparatively soft and scratches easily, which means that when installed as a glazing material it must be treated with care. On the other hand acrylic will not shatter like glass and is a better thermal insulator.

In America, following John Ott's work, ultraviolet transmitting plastic is also available for glasses and contact lenses. A company in California offers 'full-spectrum' lenses for glasses and most common prescription lenses are held in stock. A 'neutral density' grey coloured plastic lens for prescription sunglasses is also available. This special filter evenly reduces the transmission of all visible and near-ultraviolet wavelengths, unlike most sunglasses — even with grey lenses these often transmit several marked peaks of energy which only *look* grey. Two other manufacturers in America are

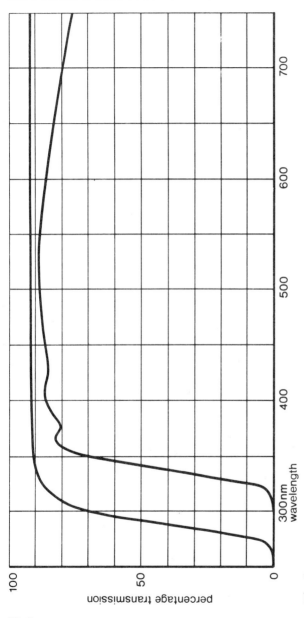

Fig. 5

The transmission curves for clear glass and ultraviolet-transmitting acrylic. These two curves show the degree to which the two materials are transparent at different wavelengths. The inner curve is for 6mm float glass and the outer curve is for quarter inch (6.35mm) 'plexiglass'. The curves for float glass and sheet glass are similar.

making 'full-spectrum' clear plastic contact lenses which specifically transmit near-ultraviolet.

Any glass, in windows or in glasses, which has a coloured tint or has been covered with plastic or metallised film of any kind, is probably substantially distorting the wavelength distribution of natural daylight — even in the case of clear film, since it is usually made of polyester, which is vulnerable to ultraviolet damage and has a screening additive for protection. Nevertheless, ordinary clear glass currently remains more practical than acrylic for window glazing in most cases; the thicker it is though, the more it will attenuate the ultraviolet.

If we take the trouble to use the best glazing material, can it be assumed that we can rely on daylight to be in its 'natural' condition? Air pollution, especially in cities, is not new. When soft coal was introduced in England around 1650, rickets appeared for the first time and then spread throughout Europe with the Industrial Revolution. Although most of us no longer live under a pall of coal smoke there are many invisible pollutants in the air over our major cities which absorb ultraviolet. What is known as 'photochemical smog' — which forms as a faint white haze — is fairly common when the sun shines and the air is still. Thus the daylight that reaches us may be altered from its natural condition. Taken together with the fact that in our industrial culture there is a predominance of indoor activity, this means that we still need to rely on artificial light as a substitute for the exposure to unfiltered daylight which we would otherwise have received, with whatever benefits might have been conferred.

Leaving aside such things as candles and lasers, there are two ways of generating artificial light for general use: incandescence and gas discharge. The ordinary light bulb is an example of incandescent light and the fluorescent tube of gas discharge light. The colour output needs careful adjustment if artificial light is to resemble daylight.

Incandescence is the release of heat and light when an object is raised to bright red heat or above. Incandescent lamps consist of a fine tungsten wire sealed into a glass bulb; when the wire carries an electric current at the intended voltage it becomes white hot. In ordinary light bulbs the filament runs at about 2500°C which gives a relatively 'yellowish' white light. Temperatures above about 3200°C are currently not feasible (even with a special gas filling as in tungsten halogen lamps). Practical filament materials which would run at higher temperatures have not been developed, and the lamp itself would become impractically hot.

The light emitted at higher incandescent temperatures becomes progressively whiter and finally bluish, and this has led to the adoption of a yardstick called 'colour temperature'. Daylight, taking the light from the sun and sky together, varies between a colour temperature of 5500°K and 6500°K: in other words it is the same colour as the light given off by an object around five or six thousand degrees centigrade. (Colour temperatures are expressed in degrees Kelvin — they are the same magnitude as degrees centigrade but the scale starts at minus 273°C, the lowest theoretically attainable temperature).

But what do we see as 'white'? In 1951 Hurvich and Jameson reported that studies in which a white magnesium oxide surface was illuminated with a succession of different 'white' lights had demonstrated that light with a colour temperature of 5500° K was seen as true white. Above this the surface looked bluish, and at lower temperatures it looked yellowish. In other words, our visual system, in spite of its tolerance of colour shifts, does seem to take the lower value of the daylight range as a neutral point, which is a further indication of our adaptation to natural light. It also seems appropriate to choose this value to define full-spectrum light since it thus meets both visual and non-visual requirements.

Although the ordinary incandescent lamp cannot operate at temperatures as high as 5500° K, it is possible to increase the effective colour temperature by colouring the glass envelope with a clear blue tint which reduces the yellowness of the light. In a number of countries such 'daylight' incandescent bulbs are easily available, but in others, such as England, they can only be obtained from specialist suppliers. Unfortunately they are neither efficient nor wholly effective as a source of full-spectrum light since they are very low in energy at the blue end of the spectrum and they give negligible amounts of near-ultraviolet.

Higher effective colour temperatures are much more efficiently achieved by using gas discharge light sources. There are many different types of gas discharge lamp, but they all work in the same way. Gas, at either high or low pressure, is trapped in a glass, quartz or ceramic tube which has a metal electrode sealed into each end. When a sufficiently high voltage is connected across these electrodes, the gas atoms or molecules become ionized, releasing electrons which then permit an electric current to flow. When this happens the gas atoms repeatedly become energized by electron collisions and repeatedly release this energy as radiation, generally as visible light or ultraviolet. The discharge gas is usually the vapour of a volatile metal, most commonly mercury or sodium, and the electronic structure of its atoms determines the characteristic wavelengths which will be emitted by the diffuse glow discharge.

The most common gas discharge lamp is the fluorescent tube. It is made of glass and contains mercury vapour at low pressure, which produces most of its discharge energy in the far-ultraviolet as a very intense 'spike' of radiation at 253.7 nm. (This invisible and harmful high energy *far*-ultraviolet band is not present in daylight). The whole of the inside surface of the glass tube is coated with a mixture of powdered phosphors which 'fluoresce': they absorb the ultraviolet and re-emit its energy as visible light. As a result, fluorescent lamps can give a wide variety of colours (*see Fig. 6*) and with careful phosphor selection can mimic incandescent radiation at any desired colour temperature.

The full-spectrum fluorescent tubes manufactured in New Jersey have a colour temperature of 5500° K — but run cool enough to touch, as do all fluorescent tubes. They also have a 'blacklight' phosphor to provide the near-ultraviolet component which is present in daylight. Although the amount of ultraviolet in daylight varies more than the distribution of visible light (near-ultraviolet intensity increases the higher the sun is in the sky), a representative level for these tubes has been arrived at by relating it to the minimum erythemal

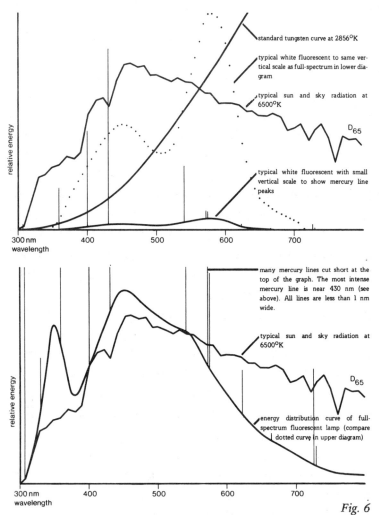

standard tungsten curve at 2856°K

typical white fluorescent to same vertical scale as full-spectrum in lower diagram

typical sun and sky radiation at 6500°K

D₆₅

typical white fluorescent with small vertical scale to show mercury line peaks

many mercury lines cut short at the top of the graph. The most intense mercury line is near 430 nm (see above). All lines are less than 1 nm wide.

typical sun and sky radiation at 6500°K

D₆₅

energy distribution curve of full-spectrum fluorescent lamp (compare dotted curve in upper diagram)

relative energy

300 nm
wavelength

400

500

600

700

Fig. 6

Artificial lighting spectra in comparison with daylight. Both diagrams show the energy distribution in daylight (the CIE standard distribution D_{65}). This spectral profile has had various statistical operations performed on it: the real thing varies constantly within fairly narrow limits and is 'spikier' than this indicates. The solid curve close to the horizontal axis of the upper graph has had its vertical scale deliberately compressed to show the true relative heights of the mercury lines.

dose referred to previously (Thorington, Parascandola and Cunningham, 1971). These full-spectrum tubes do not give such a 'cold' light as the specialist 'colour matching' tubes, which usually have a colour temperature around 6500° K, although it may well be that the latter are equally satisfactory from the photobiological point of view if they also include a near-ultraviolet component.

The majority of fluorescent lamps in use have relatively low colour temperatures between 3000° K and 4000° K. In part, this is because the lighting industry bases its assessment of lamp efficiency on the overall spectral sensitivity of the visual system, using a measure called 'efficacy'. Thus a lamp which emitted only yellow-green light at 555 nm, the wavelength to which the eye is most sensitive, would have the highest possible 'efficacy', although it would have completely sacrificed 'colour rendering' ability. The low pressure sodium vapour lamp very nearly fulfils this condition. It produces nearly all its radiation directly in the visible spectrum in two narrow spectral 'lines' at 589 nm and 589.6 nm, which means it gives an entirely monochromatic yellow-orange light. This is familiar from its use as street lighting and in similar applications where economy is considered more important than aesthetics. (It is curious that precisely these two spectral 'lines' which we use to light our streets do not appear in sunlight at all: sodium in the sun's atmosphere absorbs these two wavelengths, leaving two dark lines in the daylight spectrum at this point). Using efficacy to gauge economy certainly results in a bright light, but it is a very crude way of assessing the visual information given by a certain consumption of electricity, and makes no allowance for the possible non-visual side-effects of illumination by such a narrow band of wavelengths. Visual information is given by diversity of colour, not merely by the intensity of light at the wavelengths to which we are most sensitive, and there is already formal evidence supporting this. During the 1960's Aston and Bellchambers (Aston and Bellchambers, 1969; Lemaigre-Voreaux, 1970) demonstrated that fluorescent lamps which produce a wider and more even range of visible colours actually give better 'visual clarity' for the same power consumption than tubes with a higher efficacy. Thus efficacy compromises not only physiological responses but also vision, since it fails to provide better visual performance for a given consumption of electricity. The biological parameter on which efficacy is based was determined in the 1920's (the sensitivity of the human eye to daylight light levels was agreed internationally in 1924). Perhaps we should now consider replacing it with a new photobiological criterion.

The light produced by fluorescent tubes does still suffer from two drawbacks. There are currently no fluorescent phosphors which match the red emission of an incandescent source, so that the light from fluorescent tubes, including full-spectrum tubes, is relatively deficient at the red end of the spectrum. Also, 'lines' from the mercury vapour discharge appear in the light output. The mercury discharge, in addition to generating energy in the far-ultraviolet, emits subsidiary 'spikes' of energy in the visible and near-ultraviolet. These 'lines' consist of very intense light over a very narrow wavelength range which our visual system cannot distinguish from the rest of the light output — the lines are only visible in a spectrum of the light output. Whether they have any biological effect has not been determined. There are many emission and absorption lines in both candlelight and daylight, but these mercury lines are very intense in comparison with the phosphor output and the possibility of an adverse biological response is worth examining.

Some higher pressure discharge lamps, however, can generate light without these drawbacks and show some promise for generating a more faithful full-spectrum light. Increasing the gas pressure in a discharge lamp has the effect of broadening its primary output of radiation by spreading the energy of the emission lines over a wider range of wavelengths.

The high pressure sodium lamp cannot yet give a full-spectrum output: instead it produces a strange golden-pink light at the pressure which gives greatest efficacy. In fact a high pressure sodium vapour discharge produces its best colour — comparable to tungsten halogen — at gas pressures between 450 Torr and 500 Torr, but the inferior colour at 100 Torr to 200 Torr is used because of its higher efficacy. It is significant that in some cases where these lamps have been installed in interiors in America there has been a strong adverse reaction. The Fort Worth School District in Texas, for example, was obliged to remove high pressure sodium lamps from classrooms following considerable discomfort and complaint among both teachers and pupils (Evans, 1977; Mills and Anderson, 1980; also Flynn, 1977; Ronchi, 1978 - adverse visual effects).

In the case of the high pressure mercury vapour discharge

lamp there is the prospect of making a very good full-spectrum light indeed. As the vapour pressure of a mercury discharge is increased it radiates much less energy in the ultraviolet and progressively more in the visible. The spectral lines are increasingly broadened and spectrally continuous radiation is emitted. In this form the colour rendering is not particularly good, but the addition of metal halides to the discharge gas substantially improves the colour output. A variety of different metal halides are used, but lamps with thallium, indium and dysprosium iodides give a more or less continuous spectral output right across the visible range including the near-ultraviolet. They are closer to a daylight distribution than the full spectrum fluorescent tubes, but at the time of writing are only available at relatively high power levels of several hundred watts. Even closer approximations to daylight have been achieved in experimental lamps containing thallium, dysprosium, holmium and thulium iodides. Given further development, the metal halide lamp should be the most practical way of generating a full-spectrum light genuinely close to daylight.

The remaining full-spectrum contender is the xenon gas discharge lamp. The compact-source xenon arc is extremely bright and is the only known source which closely resembles sunlight in spectral output and intensity. It gives excellent colour rendering and has a colour temperature of 5600° K. These lamps are used for sports floodlighting and projectors, but have certain disadvantages: they are expensive, very occasionally explode and require bulky electrical running gear. As a result they are only infrequently used for interior lighting and are unlikely to be a practical full-spectrum source except for large scale applications, for which they would be ideal. They are reported to be used in Russia to provide photobiologically effective lighting in factories and workshops.

Discharge lamps are the obvious choice for providing a photobiologically satisfactory source of light for general use both because of the type of light they can produce and because they represent a very efficient conversion of electrical energy into visible radiation, which means they are cheap to run. Fluorescent lamps, for example, use only about one third the power of tungsten lamps, and generate relatively little unwanted heat — which explains why they are in such widespread use. Nevertheless, in their present form, discharge lamps do have certain disadvantageous side-effects. These seem to be particularly apparent in fluorescent lamps. In high pressure compact lamps they either do not apply to the same extent or are easier to rectify.

Discharge lamps require accessory electrical running gear to preheat the electrode filaments to provide an instantaneous high voltage to strike the discharge and to limit the operating current. Electrically, the simplest way to do this is with the mains alternating current power supply, which means that the discharge itself stops and restarts 100 or 120 times a second (depending on whether the mains frequency is 50 Hz or 60 Hz), giving the light a very fast flicker. The fact that the mains current is continually changing direction (alternating) is largely masked in an incandescent lamp because the filament stays hot while the current is reversing and the light output falls very little, at most acquiring a 'ripple' of about 10% of the total light (depending on the filament thickness) which is too small to be visible. In the case of a fluorescent lamp the 100% flicker of the discharge itself is modified to some extent by the phosphors, and the depth of the flicker or ripple is about 20% for the long wavelength phosphors, which continue to glow after the energizing radiation has stopped, but can be as much as 80% for the bluer phosphors. The current 'flows' from each end of the tube alternately, and as this happens a slower 50th or 60th of a second flicker is produced at the ends of the tube, but this is only a small part of the total light output (1-3%).

When a fluorescent tube is relatively new and is working properly, the overall flicker cannot consciously be seen by most people, particularly older people, and so is generally considered unimportant. Nevertheless, a significant number of people do find fluorescent light unpleasant, and there is anecdotal evidence that it contributes to the onset of epilepsy and migraine, these adverse reactions very often being attributed to the flicker (Mullis, 1978). Little evidence is available and it is far from conclusive. In 1967 Popescu and Gradina made a comparison of visual parameters after three hours of close work under incandescent lighting, fluorescent lighting run on alternating current, and fluorescent run on direct current. The incandescent light was significantly better than both fluorescent conditions (an interesting finding in itself), and the alternating current lamp was better than the direct current lamp, which was presumably flickerless although details of the circuit were not given. There may perhaps be some acquired tolerance to flicker, since a lowered sensitivity of this kind has been suggested in habitual television viewing (Corbett and White, 1976). On the other hand, in 1975 Brundrett reported a significant correlation between the ability to see flicker and the incidence of headaches and eyestrain among office workers.

The retina is able to follow flicker up to at least forty pulses a second, and if the light is sufficiently intense at rates well above this. In contrast, the apparent rate — the rate which is perceived — seems to level off at about six to eight pulses a second (Haber and Hershenson, 1973). In other words, although faster flicker is unconsciously seen, it does not appear to flicker at its true rate. Faster rates of flicker, however, are known to produce non-visual effects which depend on their true rate. Flicker between 8 and 13 pulses a second produced by a strobe lamp is able to induce EEG alpha rhythms in the same frequency range, so even faster rates of flicker — perhaps rates too fast to be visible — may have some effect on electrical rhythms in the brain. If this is the case, fluorescent lamp flicker may well have effects of the sort attributed to it. Certainly, whenever flicker is actually seen it is considered objectionable, so steps towards its elimination would seem desirable.

There are a number of ways of avoiding flicker in discharge lamps. The most fundamental is to run the discharge on fully smoothed direct current so that there is no break or change in the light at all. Another approach, which has been tried in various European countries, is to run adjacent tubes on circuitry which shifts the mains phase, or timing of the current alternation, in one of the two tubes. This masks the flicker by causing it to occur at slightly displaced times in the two tubes — in other words, when one tube is momentarily dark the other tube is bright, and vice versa. Herbst (1968) reported that this has succeeded in improving work performance and possibly visual acuity when the two lamps share an efficient diffuser merging their light output. Yet another alternative is to use electronic running gear with a high frequency alternating current output which may be between 5 kilohertz (one thousand Hertz, abbreviated as kHz) and 20 kHz; at such high rates of alternation the phosphors glow for long enough to completely 'fill in' the flicker. All these methods have their technical and economic pros and cons, each is feasible, but none are in general use. The electronic running gear is likely to be adopted anyway because it uses less power and makes the lamp more efficient, thus satisfying the growing call for energy-saving.

Unfortunately the light emitted is not the only thing that flickers. The running gear and the alternating discharge also cause the production of radio frequency electromagnetic radiation, which occurs in pulses at the instants of decay and initiation of the discharge and during the discharge itself. In fluorescent fixtures with standard running gear (it may be worse in high frequency units) the radiation is in the short, medium and long bands between 100 kHz and 10 megahertz (one million Hertz, abbreviated as MHz), and particularly occurs in older tubes. Much of it is radiated after conduction away from the lamp along mains wiring, which acts as an aerial; capacitors or chokes can be fitted in the control gear to reduce this. Direct radiation from the tube and fixture can only be eliminated by fitting an earthed mesh screen around the whole assembly, but this is normally only considered necessary when sensitive apparatus is within a few metres of the lamp (Henderson, 1972).

Of course life itself is comprised of sensitive systems, many of which go beyond the grasp of our present science. So it is perhaps not surprising to find that adverse biological responses to non-light fluorescent tube radiation have been reported (Martin and Gonzalez, 1976; Mayron, 1976). The effects of low levels of radio frequency energy on life are by no means clear, but it has been observed that exposing animals to UHF fields results in an accumulation of acetylcholine along nerve fibres (Mayron, 1970). This may account for aspects of the behaviour of these animals, which at first show hyperactivity followed later by a reduction in activity and increasing lethargy if the irradiation is sustained. A mild influence of this type in response to the radiofield of fluorescent lamps and fixtures cannot be entirely discounted.

It is also known that modulated radio fields at low energy levels can have an effect on brain function. The most striking evidence we have for this — but it is not suggested as a discharge lamp side-effect — is the ability we have to 'hear' directly, inside our heads, electromagnetic energy in a frequency range between 200MHz and 3000MHz when the energy is modulated in some way — in other words when it ripples or flickers. This little-known phenomenon is termed radiosound and has been studied in detail by Allan Frey (Frey and Messenger, 1973; or Battocletti, 1976).

But more relevant is the work of Ross Adey at the Veteran's Administration Hospital in Loma Linda, California. Using 147MHz radio fields modulated at frequencies the brain itself generates — in this case between 2Hz and 14Hz

— and at very low energy levels close to the EEG signal strength, he found that the behaviour of cat's brains could be significantly altered. He also showed, using a modulated 450MHz field and isolated chick brain tissue, that the response (in this case calcium ion release from the surfaces of nerve cells) is greatest when both the power and the modulation frequency correspond to those of the brain's own EEG signals. This indicates that there is a 'power window' for this modulated high frequency radio effect at incident power densities between 0.1 milliwatts per square centimetre and 1 mW/cm^2, and a 'frequency window' between 5Hz and 30Hz (Adey, 1975 and 1977; Bawin, 1975, 1976 and 1978). In this context, the word 'window' expresses the idea that both above and below these values the effect diminishes rapidly. It is tempting to speculate that fluorescent lamps and their fixtures may sometimes generate radio signals which look enough like the brain's own signalling system to affect brain function, particularly in sensitive people. This might account for the vague or generalized symptoms that are sometimes complained of; headaches and an increased sense of mental fatigue.

One more possibility has to be added to this rather daunting list of discharge lamp side-effects — X-radiation. X-ray emission from the cathode dark space of an argon-mercury discharge (as in a fluorescent lamp) was demonstrated at a cathode fall of 400 volts, according to Emeleus in 1929; but it is not generally considered possible at the somewhat lower standard fluorescent operating voltages. It may be, however, that there is X-ray emission, particularly from the longer fluorescent tubes, which is at too low a level for measurement by our present equipment but which neverthe-less has a biological effect. John Ott reported in 1974 that he had found abnormal responses in bean plants grown under banks of fluorescent lamps, those grown under the ends of the tubes being stunted and showing reversed root tropisms — in other words their roots were growing up out of the soil. Plants grown experimentally in space show very similar responses. Ott discovered that these effects could be elimina-ted by wrapping lead foil around the ends of the tubes, but not when aluminium foil was used, which led him to suggest that X-rays were responsible.

Ott acted on these observations in the Sarasota class-room experiment described earlier. All the full-spectrum tubes and fixtures were completely enclosed in earthed metal cages and the ends of the tubes were wrapped in lead foil to eliminate the effects of any stray radiation, so the experiment should properly be considered as examining both the effects of different light spectra, and the response to overall fluorescent fixture radiation. It may well be that the reduction in hyperactivity observed was a response to the removal of non-light wavelengths produced by the stan-dard fixtures. In this connection it is interesting to note that Ott has informally demonstrated a reduction of muscle strength on exposure to the radio frequency field of fluores-cent fixtures (1979). New and more systematically designed long-term studies are obviously needed to establish the rela-tive importance of such non-light radiation.

This survey of artificial lighting has focused on light sources which are already available or under development. Of course, other variations are likely to appear. At the time of writing various lamp manufacturers are introducing miniature fluorescent or low-wattage discharge lamp replacements for standard tungsten filament bulbs. With the right phosphors or discharge gas mixtures these lamps could obviously be made to give a full-spectrum output, and indeed offer the possibility of generating full-spectrum light in many kinds of ordinary domestic light fixtures. Development of these and other new light sources will certainly continue. In time fundamentally new types of light source will presumably emerge, capable possibly of even better full-spectrum output than currently exists. Perhaps there will even be lamps which could have their colour output continuously and precisely varied, to allow a true simulation of natural daylight conditions.

Meanwhile, the various side-effects of the lamps which have been described can all be eliminated using techniques which are well understood, so it would now be relatively simple to design discharge lamp running gear giving a flickerless lamp output, incorporated in fixtures which would be fully shielded to suppress non-light radiation. Fixtures of this kind, incorporating the best possible sources of full-spectrum light, should now be made available. This step would allow further research into and assessment of the many ideas and observations advanced in this book, and also permit widespread enjoyment of the potential benefits with the least possible delay.

Conclusion

This book has presented three principal sets of findings in a sequence: firstly, light does affect us physiologically, it modifies our internal chemistry; secondly, colour plays a part in this physiological response; and thirdly, the practical corollary of the first two, the most healthy condition for us appears to be illumination with light which has the same colour distribution as daylight.

When put in this context, I believe the third proposition becomes a powerful hypothesis. However surprising this may be, it is clear that daylight plays an organising or determining role in the body which we have only recently begun to uncover. Much of the material presented here needs further corroboration and analysis, but there is wide scope for immediate new research within the framework of this hypothesis.

It is hard to overestimate the importance of these findings. It is most probable that existing artificial lighting is placing large numbers of people under additional stress in an already stressful society. If it is within our power to avoid this simply by choosing artificial lighting with discrimination, then it is our responsibility to do so — even before the matter is explored further. The evidence we already have fully justifies such action.

We do not know how different aspects of *daylight* differ

in importance, but until we do it seems entirely reasonable to adopt daylight in total as the yardstick for high-quality lighting. We can be virtually certain it is safe, since it is the natural condition to which we are adapted. At the very least it would now be prudent to instal 'full-spectrum', shielded lighting fixtures in all those places where people spend most of their time, particularly working areas already lit by fluorescent lamps.

The evidence presented here suggests that there will be real benefits to health, morale and working ability. And these personal benefits will translate into social and economic benefits, not just for individual enterprises, but for our whole community.

By improving the quality of our light, we can contribute fundamentally to the future health of mankind.

References

Adey, W.R. (1975) Functional linkage in biomolecular systems *in* Evidence for cooperative mechanisms in the susceptibility of cerebral tissue to environmental and intrinsic electric fields. Biomolecular Systems, Schmitt, F.O. et al (Eds.) Raven Press, New York.

Adey, W.R. (1977) Models of membranes of cerebral cells as substrates for information storage. BioSystems, 8, 163-178.

Allen, R.M. and Cureton, T.K. (1945) Effect of ultraviolet radiation on physical fitness. Archives of physical medicine and rehabilitation, 26, 641-644.

Allen, F. and Schwartz, M. (1940) The effect of stimulation of the senses of vision, hearing, taste and smell upon the sensibility of the organs of vision. Journal of General Physiology.

Aston, S.M. and Bellchambers, H.E. (1969) Illumination, colour rendering and visual clarity. Lighting Research and Technology, 1, No 4, 259-261.

Ballowitz, L.; Heller, R.; Natzchka, J. and Ott, M. (1970) The effect of blue light on infant Gunn rats. Birth Defects. 4, No 2, 106-113.

Battocletti, J.H. (1976) Electromagnetism, Man and the Environment. Elek.

Bawin, S.M.; Kaczmarek, L.K. and Adey, W.R. (1975) Effects of modulated VHF fields on the central nervous system. Annals of the New York Academy of Sciences, 247, 74-81.

Bawin, S.M. and Adey, W.R. (1976) Sensitivity of calcium binding in cerebral tissue to weak environmental electric fields oscillating at low frequency. Proc. Natl. Acad. Sci. USA, 73, No 6, 1999-2003.

Bawin, S.M.; Sheppard, A. and Adey, W.R. (1978) Possible Mechanisms of Weak Electromagnetic Field Coupling in Brain Tissue. Bioelectrochemistry and Bioenergetics, 5, 67-76.

Bawin, S.M.; Adey, W.R. and Sabbot, I.M. (1978) Ionic factors in release of $^{45}Ca^{2+}$ from chicken cerebral tissue by electromagnetic fields. Proc. Natl. Acad. Sci. USA, 75, No 12, 6314-6318.

Becher, H. (1953) Über ein vegetatives, zentralnervöses Kerngebiet in

der Netzhaut des Menschen und der Säugetiere. Acta Neurovege-
tativa, **8**, 21.

Becher, H. (1955) Über ein vegetatives Kerngebiet und neurosekret-
orische Leistungen der Ganglienzellen der Netzhaut. Klin. Mbl.
Augenheilk. Beih. **23**, 1.

Benoit, J. and Assenmacher, I. (1955) The control of visible radia-
tions of the gonadotropic activity of the duck hypophysis.
Recent Progress in Hormone Research, **15**, 143-164. Academic
Press, New York.

Bevan, B.M. and Zeiller, W. (1966) Ultraviolet irradiation of marine
aquaria. *See:* Ott, J.N. (1973) Health and Light, Devin Adair,
Old Greenwich, Connecticut 1966; Watkins, London & Dulverton,
1981.

Birren, F. (1950) The Psychology of Color and Color Therapy. University Books, 1950 revised 1961.

Bissonnette, T.H. and Wadlund, A.P.R. (1931) Spermatogenesis in
sturnus vulgaris: refractory period and acceleration in relation to
wavelength and rate of increase of light ration. Journal of Mor-
phology and Physiology.

Bissonnette, T.H. (1933) Light and sexual cycles in starlings and fer-
rets. Quart. Rev. Biol. **8**, 201-208.

Bissonnette, T.H. and Csech, A.G. (1939) Modified sexual photope-
riodicity in cottontail rabbits. Biological Bulletin.

Bissonnette, T.H. (1941) Experimental modification of breeding
cycles in goats. Physiological Zoology.

Blinzley, R.J. and Hafley, W.L. (1966) Some biological responses of a
rat colony to artificial illumination. Animal Care Panel 17th
Annual Meeting, Chicago.

Bowen, E.J. (1965) Recent progress in Photobiology (4th Int. Photobio. Cong. Oxford 1964). Blackwell, Oxford, 1965.

Bradley, M.O. and Sharkey, N.A. (1977) Mutagenicity and toxicity of
visible fluorescent light to cultured mammalian cells. Nature, **266**.

Brodeur, P. (1976) The Zapping of America. W.W. Norton 1976.

Brundrett. G.W. (1975) Fusion criteria — a new parameter for lighting maintenance. Electricity Council Research Centre, ECRC/
M875, Job 025, December 1975.

Callahan, P.S. (1975) Tuning in to Nature. Devin Adair, Old Greenwich, Connecticut 1975; Routledge, London 1977.

Cardinali, D.P.; Larin, F. and Wurtman, R.J. (1972) Action Spectra
for effects of light on hydroxyindole-O-methyl transferases in rat
pineal, retina and harderian gland. Endocrinology, **91**, No 4.

Chance, R.E. (1978) The effects of environmental light on human performance and fitness. Thesis *for* Florida Technological University.

Cheng, M.F. (1976) Interaction of light and other environmental variables on activity of the hypothalamic hypophyseal gonadal system. Nature, 263, 148-149.

Copley, G.J. (1979) Personal Communication. Research and Development Laboratories, Pilkington Brothers Limited.

Corbett, J.M. and White, T.A. (1976) Visibility of flicker in television pictures. Nature, 261, 689-690.

Cremer, R.J.; Perryman, P.W. and Richards, D.H. (1958) Influence of light on the hyperbilirubinaemia of infants. Lancet, 1, 1094.

Critchlow, V. (1963) The role of light in the neuroendocrine system. Recent Advances in Neuroendocrinology (proc. of 1st Symp. Miami) 377-402. Univ. of Illinois Press, Urbana.

Dantsig, N.M.; Lazarev, D.N. and Sokolov, M.V. (1967) Ultra-violet installations of beneficial action. Commission Internationale de l'Éclairage, Compte Rendu 16th Session, Washington, June 1967. CIE Publication No 14A (1968).

Dejardin, G. and Falgon, R. (1954) Sur le 'papillotement' des lampes à fluorescence. Proc. 1st Int. Photobio. Cong. H. Veenman & Sons, Wageningen.

Deutsch, F. (1937) Psycho-physical reactions of the vascular system to the influence of light and to impression gained through light. Folia Clinica Orientalia, 1, Fasc 3 & 4.

Ehrenwald, H. (1932) Über einen Photo-Dermatischen Tonusreflex auf Bestrahlung mit farbigen Lichtern beim Menschen. Klin. Wchnschr., 11, 2142.

Ehrenwald, H. (1933) Über den Strahlensinn des Menschen. Klin. Wchnschr., 12, 1473.

Elenbaas, W. (1971) Fluorescent Lamps. Macmillan, London.

Ellinger, F. (1957) Medical Radiation Biology. Charles Thomas.

Emeleus, K.G. (1929) The Conduction of Electricity through Gases. Methuen.

Evans, C.L. (1977) High pressure sodium light study: Fort Worth Independent School District. Department of Research and Evaluation, Fort Worth Independent School District, Fort Worth, Texas. Spring 1977.

Epel, B.L. (1973) Inhibition of growth and respiration by visible and near visible light. Photophysiology, 8, 209-229.

Feller, R.P.; Edmonds, E.J.; Shannon, I.L. and Madsen, K.O. (1974)

Significant effect of environmental lighting on caries incidence in the cotton rat. Proceedings of the Society for Experimental Biology and Medicine, **145**, 1065-1068.

Feré, *see* Birren, F. (1950) The Psychology of Color and Color Therapy, 130, University Books, revised 1961.

Flynn, J.E. and Spencer, T.J. (1977) The effects of light source colour on user impression and satisfaction. Journal of IES, 167-179. Illuminating Engineering Society, New York.

Frey, A.H. and Messenger, R. Jr. (1973) Human perception of illumination with pulsed ultra-high frequency electromagnetic energy. Science, **181**, 356-358.

Gage, H.P. (1930) Hygenic Effects of Ultraviolet Radiation in Daylight. Trans. IES, **25**, 377.

Gerard, R.M. (1958) Differential effects of colored lights on psychophysiological functions. Unpublished doctoral dissertation, University of California, Los Angeles, California.

Giessmann, H.G. and Lindner, H. (1974) Influence of the level of lighting on concentration. Arbeitsmed. Fragen in der Opthalmologie, 4, 108-114.

Glucksmann, A. (1978) Sex Determination and Sexual Dimorphism in Mammals. Wykeham Publications, London.

Goldstein, K. (1942) Some experimental observations concerning the influence of colour on the function of the organism. Occupational Therapy and Rehabilitation.

Greiter, F.; Guttman, G. and Bachi, N. (1979) 7th Annual Meeting of the American Society for Photobiology, Pacific Grove, California.

Haber, R.N. and Hershenson, M. (1973) The Psychology of Visual Perception. Holt, Rinehart and Winston.

Halpern, L. and Feinmesser, M. (1956) The variability of threshold of acoustic discomfort in sensorimotor induction syndrome with special reference to the effect of colours. Confin. Neurol. Basel, 75, 309-320.

Halpern, L. (1956) Additional contributions to the sensorimotor induction syndrome in unilateral disequilibrium with special reference to the effect of colours. J. Nerv. Ment. Dis., **123**, 334-350.

Harrison, P.; McGinnis, J.; Schumaier, G. and Lauber, J. (1969) Sexual maturity and subsequent reproductive performance of white leghorn chickens subjected to different parts of the light spectrum. Poultry Science, **48**, 878-883.

Henderson, S.T. and Marsden, A.M. (1972) Lamps and Lighting, Arnold 1972.

Herbst, C.H. (1968) The effect of light on workers. Elektrizität, 11, 294-300.

Himmelfarb, P.; Scott, A. and Thayer, P.S. (1970) Bactericidal activity of a broad spectrum illumination source. Applied Microbiology, June 1970, 1013-1014.

Hodr, R. (1971) Phototherapy of hyperbilirubinaemia in premature infants. Ceskoslovenska Pediatrie, 26, 80-82.

Hoffman, see Birren, F. (1950).

Hollwich, F, and Tilgner, S. (1961) Experimentelle Untersuchingen über den Einfluss monochromatischen Lichtes auf die Hodenentwicklung des Erples. Klin. Mbl. Augenheilk. 139, 828-835.

Hollwich, F. (1979) The Influence of Ocular Light Perception on Metabolism in Man and in Animal. Springer-Verlag, New York.

Hurvich, L.M. and Jameson, D. (1951) J. Opt. Soc. Amer., 41, 521.

Hurvich, L.M. and Jameson, D. (1951) J. Opt. Soc. Amer., 41, 787.

Hurvich, L.M. and Jameson, D. (1957) An opponent-process theory of colour vision. Psychological Review, 64, 384-404.

Jacobson, E.D.; Krell, K.; Dempsey, M.J.; Lugo, M.H.; Ellingson, O. and Hench, C.W. II (1978). Toxicity and mutagenicity of radiation from fluorescent lamps and a sunlamp in L5178Y mouse lymphoma cells. Mutation Research, 51, 61-75.

Jaffe, M.J. (1970) Evidence for the regulation of phytochrome-mediated processes in bean roots by the neurohormone, acetylcholine. Plant Physiol., 46, 768.

Jagger, J. (1967) Introduction to research in ultraviolet photobiology. Prentice-Hall, New Jersey.

Jewess, B.W. (1978) Medical uses of radiation from lamps. IES/CIBS National Lighting Conference 1978, G1-G8.

Judd, D.B. (1965) Spectral distribution of typical daylight as a function of correlated color temperature. Illuminating Engineering, LX, No 4, Sec 1, 272-278.

Kalich, J. (1962) Wissenschaftliche Untersuchungen im Dienste der modernen 'Hühnerfarm'. Umschau, 62, 741.

Kappers, J.A.; Smith, A.R. and De Vries, R.A.C. (1974) The mammalian pineal gland and its control of hypothalamic activity. Prog. Brain Res. 41, 170-173.

Karacevceva, T.V. (1971) The role of UV radiation as part of modern methods of treating and preventing rheumatism in children, in Ultraviolet radiation. Medicina, Moscow, 154-158.

Kennedy, A.; Little, J. and Ritter, M. (1980) Science, 207, 1209-1211.

Kerenyi, N.A. (1977) The pineal gland — what is its true importance? Modern Medicine, 81-84, Nov. 1977.

Kinsey, V.E. (1948) Spectral Transmission of the Eye to Ultraviolet Radiation. Arch. Opth. 39, 508.

Klein, E. and Weis, V. (1953) Statische Untersuchungen über die Steigerung der Leistungsfähigkeit durch UV-Bestrahlung. Arbeitsphysiologie, 15, 85.

Kline Chinchilla Research Foundation, Utica, Illinois. Report on effect of light on sex ratios. April 1970.

Korbel, S. and Thompson, W.D. (1965) Behavioural effects of stimulation by UHF radio fields. Psychological Reports, 17, 595-602.

Kravkov, S. V. (1942) Color vision and autonomic nervous system. Journal of the Optical Society of America, June 1942.

Kravkov, S.V. and Galochkina, L.P. (1947) Effect of a constant current on vision. Journal of the Optical Society of America. March 1947.

Kueter, K.E. and Ott, J.N. (1964) Effects of light on animals. 15th Annual Meeting of Animal Care, 1964.

Kunitsyna, L.A.; Yezhova, V.A.; Cerfus, I.S.; Pertsovskiy, A.I. and Sarzhisko, Y.M. (1977) Clinical-physiological basis for application of longwave ultraviolet irradiation in the complex therapy of patients with early cerebral atherosclerosis with temporary disturbance of cerebral circulation. Voprosy Kurortologii, Fizioterapii i Lechebnoi Fizicheskoi Kultury, 5.

Land, E.H. (1977) The Retinex Theory of Color Vision. Scientific American, 237, No 6, Dec. 1977.

Laszlo, J. (1969) Observations on two new artificial lights for reptile displays. International Zoo Yearbook, 9, 12-13, Zoological Soc. of London.

Lehmann, G. and Szakall, A. (1932) Der Einfluss der Ultraviolettbestrahlung auf den Arbeitsstoffwechsel und die Arbeitsfähigkeit des Menschen. Arbeitsphysiologie, 5, 278.

Lemaigre-Voreaux, P. (1970) In favour of 'de luxe' fluorescent lamps. Lux, 60, 564-565.

Llewellyn, L.J. (1932) Light and sexual periodicity. Nature, 868.

Loomis, W.F. (1970) Rickets. Scientific American, 223, No 6, 77-91.

Lucey, J.F. (1972) Neonatal jaundice and phototherapy. Pediatric Clinics of North America, 19, No 4.

Ludwig and von Ries, see Prescott, B.D. (1942) The Psychological analysis of light and color. Occupational Therapy and Rehabilitation.

Luscher, M. (1970) The Luscher Colour Test. Cape, 1970.

Maas, J.B.; Jayson, and Kleiber. (1974) Effects of spectral differences in illumination on fatigue. Journal of Applied Psychology, 59, 524-526.

Magnus, I.A. (1976) Dermatological Photobiology. Blackwell, Oxford.

Martin, D.F. and Gonzalez, M.H. (1976) Artificial initiation of sessile forms of the red tide organism gymnodinium breve. J. Environ. Sci. Health, A11(6), 385-395.

Mayron, L.W. (1970) Environmental pollution: its biological effects and impact on the bioanalytical laboratory. Paper given at American Association for the Advancement of Science Meeting, Chicago, December 1970.

Mayron, L.W.; Ott, J.; Nations, R. and Mayron, E.L. (1974) Light, radiation and academic behaviour. Academic Therapy, X, No 1, 33-47.

Mayron, L.W.; Ott, J.N.; Amontree, E.J. and Nations, R. (1975) Light, radiation and dental caries. Academic Therapy, X, No 4, 441-448.

Mayron, L.W.; Ott, J.N.; Amontree, E.J. and Nations, R. (1975) Caries reduction in school children. Applied Radiology/Nuclear Medicine, July/August 1975.

Mayron, L.W. and Kaplan, E. (1976) Bioeffects of fluorescent lighting. Academic Therapy, XII, No 1.

Maughan, G.H. and Smiley, D.F. (1929) Irradiations from a quartz mercury vapour lamp as a factor in the control of common colds. Am. J. Hyg., 9, 466.

Menju, K. (1940) Effect of the visible light upon the secretion of milk. Japanese Journal of Obstetrics and Gynecology.

Metzger, A. (1925) Über das physiologische Substrat der optische-motorische Erlebniseinheit. Ber. dtsch. opthal. Ges., 45., 97-100. (Also quoted in Deutsch, F., (1937) Psycho-physical reactions of the vascular system to the influence of light and to impression gained through light).

Mills, L.F. and Andersen, F.A. (1980) Report on classroom use of Sodium Vapor Lamps. Bureau of Radiological Health Report, Rockville, Maryland, Feb. 1980.

Milroy, W.C. and Michaelson, S.M. (1972) Thyroid pathophysiology of microwave radiation. Aerosp. Med. 43, 1126-1131.

Mulder, J.D. (1960) Drug resistant malaria tertiana cured by phototherapy, in Progress in Photobiology, Elsevier, Copenhagen.

Mullis, D.R. (1978) Personal communication. Director, Migraine Trust, London WC1.

Neer, R.M.; Davis, T.R.A.; Walcott, A.; Koski, S.; Schepis, P.; Taylor, I,; Thorington, L. and Wurtman, R.J. (1971) Stimulation by artificial ligthing of calcium absorption in elderly human subjects. Nature, 229, Jan. 1971.

Neer, R.M. (1971) Paper presented at IERI Symposium, August 1971.

Ninnemann, H.; Butler, W.L. and Epel, B.L. (1970). Biochim. Biophys. Acta, 205, 507.

Nuckolls, J.L. (1976) Interior Lighting for Environmental Designers. Wiley-Interscience.

Ott, J.N. (1958) My Ivory Cellar. Twentieth Century Press.

Ott, J.N. (1964a) Some observations on the effect of light on the pigment epithelial cells of the retina of a rabbit's eye. Proc. 4th Int. Photobio. Cong. See: Bowen, E.J. (1964) Recent progress in photobiology.

Ott, J.N. (1964b) Some responses of plants and animals to variations in wavelengths of light energy. Annals of NY Acad. Sci., 117, Art. 1. See: Whipple, H.E. (1964) Photo-neuro-endocrine effects in circadian systems, with particular reference to the eye.

Ott, J.N. (1965) Effects of wavelengths of light on physiological functions of plants and animals. Illuminating Engineering, LX, No 4, Sec 1, 254-261.

Ott, J.N. (1968a) The influence of light on the retinal hypothalamic endocrine system. Annals of Dentistry, XXVII, No 1, 10-16.

Ott, J.N. (1968b) Responses of psychological and physiological functions to environmental light, Part 1, Part II, Journal of Learning Disabilities, 1, No 5, 18-20; No 6, 6-12.

Ott, J.N. (1973) Health and Light. Devin Adair, Old Greenwich, Connecticut, 1973; Pocket Books, 1976; Watkins, London & Dulverton, 1981.

Ott, J.N. (1974) The eye's dual function, Part I, II, III. The Eye, Ear, Nose and Throat Monthly, July - Nov. 1974.

Ott, J.N. (1976) Influence of fluorescent lights on hyperactivity and learning disabilities. Journal of Learning Disabilities, Aug/Sept. '76.

Ott, J.N. (1978, 1979) Personal communication.

Painter, M. (1975) Fluorescent lights and hyperactivity in children: an experiment. Press Release from County Office of Education, Santa Cruz, California.

Pertsovskiy, A.I. and Kunitsyna, L.A. (1977) Biochemical assessment of the effectiveness of different ultraviolet irradiation modes on patients with cerebral atherosclerosis. Vopr Kurortol Fizioter Lech Fiz Kult, 3, 821.

Peters, R.P.; Chapin, L.T.; Leining, K.B. and Tucker, H.A. (1978) (Light stimulated growth and milk production in cattle). Michigan State University.

Plank, J.J. and Schick, J. (1974) The effects of color on human behavior. Journal of the Association for Study in Perception, 9, 4-16.

Proceedings of the First International Photobiological Congress (4th International Light Congress). Amsterdam, Aug. 1954, H. Veenman and Sons, Wageningen.

Proceedings of 2nd International Photobiology Congress. Minerva Medical Monograph, 1957.

Progress in Photobiology, Proceedings of 3rd International Photobiology Congress, Copenhagen 1960. Elsevier 1961.

Proceedings of the 4th International Photobiology Congress. See Bowen, E.J. (1965) Recent progress in Photobiology.

Photophysiology (1964-1973) 1-8, Giese, A.C. (Ed.). Academic Press, New York.

Photochemical and Photobiological Reviews (1976 -   ) Smith, K.C. (Ed.) Plenum Press, New York.

Photochemistry and Photobiology (1962 -) Pergamon Press, London.

Pleasonton, A.J. (1877) The influence of the blue ray of the sunlight and of the blue colour of the sky, in developing animal and vegetable life; in arresting disease, and in restoring health in acute chronic disorders to human and domestic animals. Claxton, Remsen & Haffelfinger, Philadelphia.

Popescu, M.P. and Grădină, C. (1967) L'oeil dans les conditions du travail à l'éclairage fluorescent. Review Roumaine de Physiologie, 4, 155-162.

Prescott, B.D. (1942) The psychological analysis of light and color. Occupational Therapy and Rehabilitation.

Raiter, J.B. and Thut, J.F. (1976) Fluorescent lighting in schools. Environmental Research Associates 1628 - 23rd Longview WA 98632, Sept. 1976.

Rasmussen, H. and Pechet, M.M. (1970) Calcitonin. Scientific American, Oct. 1970, 42-50.

Relkin, R. (1976) The Pineal 1976. Eden Press, Montreal.

Reiter, R.J. (1977) The Pineal 1977. Eden Press, Montreal.

Ronchi, L. and Stefanacci, S. (1978) Ametropia and colour discrimination under high pressure sodium and mercury lamps. AIDI Third Lux Europa.

Ronge, H.E. (1948) Ultraviolet irradiation with artificial illumination. Acta Phyiol. Scand. (Suppl. 49), 15, 1.

Rowan, W.M. (1954) Photoperiodism in vertebrates. Proc. 1st Int. Photobio. Cong., H. Veenman and Sons, Wageningen.

Salvatori, P. (1969) *See*: Ott, J.N. (1973) Health & Light, 109, 1976 and 1981 editions.

Saltarelli, C.G. and Matteliano, J.C. (1976) The effects of different wavelengths of light on organs of Ha/ICR random bred mice. Dept. of Health, Roswell Park Memorial Institute, 666 Elm Street, Buffalo NY 14263, April 1976.

Schmidek, H.H. (1977) Pineal Tumors. Masson.

Seidl, E. (1969) The influence of ultraviolet radiation on the healthy adult. The Biologic Effects of Ultraviolet Radiation (With Emphasis on the Skin), (Ed.) F. Urbach, 447, Pergamon, Oxford.

Sery, T.W.; Pollikoff, R. and Kaczurowski, M. (1973) Comparison of Cathode-shielded, full spectrum fluorescent light vs cool white, warm white, pink and black light fluorescent on the development of Harding-Passey mouse melanoma. Wills Eye Hospital and Research Institute, Philadelphia, Pennsylvania.

Sharon, I.M.; Feller, R.P. and Burney, S.W. (1971) The effects of lights of different spectra on caries incidence in the golden hamster. Archives of Oral Biology, 16, 1427-1431.

Sherman, J.B. (1938) Prophylaxis of the common cold. Brit. M. J., 11, 903.

Shipley, T (1964) Rod-cone duplexity and the autonomic action of light. The Journ. of Vision Research, 4, Nos 1/2, 155-177.

Sinclair, J.D. (1972) Ethanol consumption in rats under different lighting conditions. Science 175, 1143-1144.

Sisson, T.R.C. (1976) Visible light therapy of neonatal hyperbilirubinaemia. Photochemical & Photobiological Reviews, 1.

Smith, K.C. (1977) The Science of Photobiology. Plenum Press.

Stein, (1910) *See*: Birren, F. (1950) The psychology of color and color therapy, 130, 1961 edition.

Teevan, R.C. and Birney, R.C. (1961) Color vision. Van Nostrand.

Thompson, A.P.D. (1951) Relation of retinal stimulation to oestrus in the ferret. J. Physiol. 113, 425.

Thorington, L.; Cunningham, L. and Parascandola, J. (1971) The illuminant in the prevention and phototherapy of hyperbilirubinaemia. Illuminating Engineering, April 1971, 240-250.

Thorington, L.; Parascandola, L. and Cunningham, L. (1971) Visual and biologic aspects of an artificial sunlight illuminant. Journal of IES, 33-41, October 1971.

Volkova, N.V. (1967) Experience in the use of erythemic ultraviolet radiation in the general lighting system of a machine shop. Higiena i Sanitariia, 32, 109-111.

Vriend, J. and Lauber, J.K. (1973) Effects of light intensity wavelength and quanta on gonads and spleen of the deer mouse. Nature, 244, 37-38.

Werner, H. (1948) Comparative psychology of mental development. Follett, Chicago.

Whipple, H.E. (Ed.) (1964) Photo-neuro-endocrine effects in circadian systems, with particular reference to the eye. Annals of the New York Academy of Sciences, 117, Art. 1, 1-645, Sept. 1964.

Wolken, J.K. (1975) Photoprocesses, Photoreceptors and Evolution. Academic Press.

Wright, J.; Galloway, C.; Sydnor, K.L.; Gabby, S.L.; Scanlon, E.F. and Ott, J.N. (1969) Special report on indicated possible relationship of light and tumor development. Environmental Health and Light Research Institute, Sarasota, Florida.

Wurtman, R.J. (1968) Biological implications of artificial illumination. Paper at National IES conference Sept. 1968, Phoenix, Arizona.

Wurtman, R.J. (1969) The pineal and endocrine function. Hospital Practice, 4, No 1, 32-37.

Wurtman, R.J. and Weisel, J. (1969) Environmental lighting and neuroendocrine function: relationship between spectrum of light source and gonadal growth. Endocrinology, 85, No 6, 1218-1221.

Wurtman, R.J. (1975) The effects of light on the human body. Scientific American, July 1975, 68-77.

Zamkova, M.A. and Krivitskaya, E.I. (1966) Effect of ultraviolet erythema lamps on the working ability of school children. Gigiena i Sanitariia, 31, 41-44.

Zietz, K. (1931) See: Werner, H. (1948) Comparative psychology of mental development.

Zilov, Ju.D. (1971) The prophylactic irradiation of children and adolescents living in different climatic zones of the Soviet Union. Ultraviolet Radiation, Moscow Medicine, 237-241.

If you have any queries regarding these references, please contact the author.